Britain Today

LONGMAN BACKGROUND BOOKS

Britain Today

Richard Musman

 Longman

LONGMAN GROUP LIMITED
London
Associated companies, branches and representatives
throughout the world

This edition © Longman Group Limited 1973, 1976

First published 1973
Second edition 1977

ISBN 0 582 55261 3

Printed in Great Britain by
J. W. Arrowsmith Ltd., Bristol, England.

BACKGROUND BOOKS

Background Books is a new series of
informative and factual books about aspects
of Britain's past and present. In many
countries students who are learning a
foreign language are required to learn also
something of the cultural activities, the
attitudes of mind and the ways of life of the
people whose language they are learning.
This series is therefore an attempt to help
the foreign student by describing and
examining certain aspects of British life and
history.

Other titles in the series are *An Outline of
English Literature*, *An Outline History of
England*, and *London Today*.

All the books in the series are written
within a general vocabulary of 2000 words
(taken from *A General Service List of English
Words*), to which the authors have added a
limited number of words outside this list
where they are connected with the subject
and facilitate expression.

Acknowledgments

We are grateful to the following for permission to reproduce the illustrations:

Aerofilms, pages 97, 161 top and bottom; ATV Network Ltd., page 178 top right, Alan Band Associates, page 76 bottom; Barnaby's Picture Library, pages 12 top and bottom, 38, 64, 90 bottom, 120 bottom, 126 top right, 133 top and bottom, 139, 166 bottom, 219 top and middle; British Broadcasting Corporation, pages 178 top left and middle, 209; British Dental Association, page 92; British Travel Association, pages 70 top, 114 top; Building Design Partnership, page 35 top; Camera Press, pages 17, 20, 26, 39 bottom right, 47, 105, 142 top and bottom, 174 bottom, 182 top, 188, 210 top and bottom, 219, bottom, 30 top; Canada House, page 224 top; J. Allan Cash, page 39 bottom left, 69, 156 top; Financial Times, page 102 bottom; Fox Photos, page 114 bottom; General Post Office, page 126 top left; Henry Grant AIIP, pages 90 top, 147 bottom; The Guardian, page 60 top and cover; Her Majesty's Stationery Office, pages 56, 114, 126 bottom; John Hillelson Agency, page 41; Keystone Press Agency, pages 23, 46, 128 bottom, 166 top, 231 top; E. D. Lacey, page 231 bottom; The Mansell Collection, page 76 top; National Portrait Gallery, page 30 middle; P.A.C.E., page 93; Popperfoto, pages 39 top, 60 bottom, 70 bottom, 128 top, 138, 149 top, 205; Press Association, page 168; Radio Times Hulton Picture Library, page 57; Rolls Royce Ltd., page 108; Alec Russell of Scarborough, page 194 bottom; SGS, pages 99, 113, 221; Shelter, page 98; Sotheby and Co., page 194 top; Sport and General Press Agency, page 193; Syndication International, page 85 bottom; Thames Television, page 178 bottom; The Times, pages 30 bottom, 71, 174 top; Topix, pages 35 bottom, 102 top, 156 bottom, 170, 182 bottom, 189; Zambia Information Service, page 224 bottom.

Map page 214 Marjorie Piggott; map page 97 Specialised Drawing Services; drawings by Edward McLachlan.

Contents

A	Avon	HA	Hampshire
AN	Antrim	HT	Hertford
AR	Armagh	HU	Humberside
B	Borders	HW	Hereford
BD	Bedford		& Worcester
BE	Berkshire	IOW	Isle of Wight
BK	Buckinghamshire	K	Kent
C	Central	L	Lothian
CA	Cambridgeshire	LA	Lancashire
CH	Cheshire	LD	Londonderry
CL	Clwyd	LE	Leicestershire
CO	Cornwall	LI	Lincoln
CU	Cumbria	M	Merseyside
CV	Cleveland	MG	Mid Glamorgan
D	Durham	N	Northumberland
DE	Derbyshire	NF	Norfolk
DG	Dumfries	NO	Nottinghamshire
	& Galloway	NT	Northampton
DO	Down	NY	N. Yorkshire
DR	Dorset	O	Orkney
DV	Devon	OX	Oxfordshire
DY	Dyfed	P	Powys
E	Essex	S	Strathclyde
ES	E. Sussex	SA	Salop
F	Fife	SG	S. Glamorgan
FE	Fermanagh	SH	Shetland
G	Grampian	SO	Somerset
GC	Gloucester	SR	Surrey
GL	Greater	ST	Staffordshire
	London	SU	Suffolk
GM	Greater	SY	S. Yorkshire
	Manchester	T	Tayside
GT	Gwent	TW	Tyne & Wear
GW	Gwynedd	TY	Tyrone
H	Highland	W	Warwick
		WG	W. Glamorgan
		WI	Western Isles
		WM	W. Midlands
		WS	W. Sussex
		WT	Wiltshire
		WY	W. Yorkshire

Great Britain and Northern Ireland: county boundaries

Introduction

Britain is changing more rapidly than ever before in her long history. In some respects the new British society reflects general world trends. In other respects it has kept its own particular flavour. British society is evolving, that is to say, developing and suiting itself to rapidly changing conditions. Evolution rather than revolution or violent change is a special characteristic of the British way of life.

This is shown in one way by how the British people vote at elections. The Conservative and Labour Parties have controlled the political scene for the last fifty years, but today neither party can any longer be sure from which class or income group its support will come. Not long ago you would have expected the working classes always to vote for the Labour Party. The word 'labour' means 'hard work'—especially hard work with the hands. The Labour Party is the party which is supposed to represent the 'working man'. You would also have expected the upper and middle classes to vote for the Conservative Party. The word 'conservative' means 'keeping things as they are'. The Conservative Party is supposed to be the party which represents property owners, businessmen and the self-employed. In some respects traditional British 'class distinctions' are becoming less clear, and you can be less sure how people will vote. Many members of the middle class support social reform. Many ordinary working people enjoy a better standard of living and are suspicious of any change which might affect them. But the old divisions between the classes remain. Many Conservatives fear that the sovereignty of Parliament is being threatened by the Trade Unions. Many workers are afraid that the Conservative bosses are trying to keep their wages down. But class feelings have not reached a personal level yet. Middle-class and working-class men can stand together at a football match and be the best of friends.

During the 1950s a Frenchman wrote: 'For nearly 900 years, safe from invasion, the island fortress of England has defended herself against ideas as if they were poisons. She has protected her way of life with a passion which to outsiders sometimes seems blind.'

Britain is no longer an island fortress. The English Channel can no longer protect her either from invasion or from the 'poison' of new ideas. The views which many foreigners have of Britain and the British are already out-of-date. So are some of the views which the British have about themselves. How then do the modern British live? What opinions do they hold about all the problems which face them, their country and the world in general?

In this book the British way of life is presented in two different ways: (1) through short, factual accounts supported by lists, graphs, diagrams and statistics, (2) through imaginary characters who represent different social backgrounds, income groups, generations, political and religious beliefs. However, the things these characters say have not been invented by the author. They are things which are being said somewhere in Britain every day of the week.

Notes
The superior figures in the text refer to the Notes at the end of each chapter. There is additional information in the Notes which is not always directly connected to the text; in these cases there are no superior figures.

Tape recordings
The dialogues from this book have been recorded. The beginning of the taped extract is marked ●, the end is marked ○.

Further reading
In some cases suggestions for further reading are given at the end of the Notes. All books are published by Penguin unless otherwise stated.

The Characters

GWYN WILLIAMS (aged 45), a factory worker
MARY WILLIAMS (43), his wife
JIM WILLIAMS (17), their youngest son—works in a fish market
GARETH WILLIAMS (18), Jim's brother—still at school
CHRISTINE (19), Gareth's girlfriend—a typist
IAN MACDONALD (28), a bank clerk
PEGGY MACDONALD (27), his wife—a secretary
SIR ERIC BLAKENEY (64), a country gentleman and managing director of an industrial firm
HESTER (LADY BLAKENEY) (55), his wife
SUSAN BLAKENEY (20), their daughter—a student
CHARLES BLAKENEY (32), their son—director in the family business
ANNE (25), his Australian wife
PENNY MARTIN (23), a friend of Susan's—a photographer's model
JEREMY MARTIN (22), Penny's brother and Susan's boyfriend—of no fixed job
HERBERT PERKINS (44), owner of a supermarket chain
CULVER JONES (50), an American friend of Charles Blakeney
CARLOS GARCIA (45), a South American friend of Charles Blakeney
GEORGE and PHYLLIS BLANDFORD, neighbours of the Blakeneys
LEONARD TOWNSEND (32), a television interviewer
ELIZABETH TOWNSEND (29), his wife—a social worker
Characters taking part in radio and television interviews and discussions with Leonard Townsend: The headmistress of a primary school, the secretary of a West Indian Association, an Indian doctor, a politician with right-wing tendencies, an American professor, a sociologist, a councillor in a new town, a chief inspector of police, a militant left-wing student, a Church of England parson, three students from three different universities, a television dramatist, the president of the 'Keep Television Clean' society, two Conservative M.P.s, two Labour M.P.s

Gwyn and Mary Williams outside their home. They live a very different life from Herbert Perkins, seen here entertaining Charles and Anne Blakeney.

I

Introducing the British

GWYN AND MARY WILLIAMS

The Williams family live in the East End of London—in a street of terraced houses called 'Royal Row'. Royal Row, built in 1863 when Queen Victoria was on the throne, is far from 'royal'. The once yellow bricks are now black with the dirt, smoke and rain of more than a hundred years. Each house has two small rooms upstairs and two rooms downstairs. There is no bathroom, and the toilet is in the backyard. All the houses in the street are due to be pulled down next year.

However, a visitor to Royal Row would be deceived by first appearances. If he looked closely at the children playing in the dusty street he would find that most of them were well dressed and well fed. Among the old second-hand cars parked outside the front doors, he would see new Minis and Volkswagens, and if Mary Williams invited him inside number 10 he would find that the brightly-flowered wallpaper, the red and orange carpets, and the shiny brown furniture all looked new and spotlessly clean.

Mary has a large china dog sitting on a table in the front room, just under the window. It looks out into the street, and at night the curtains are drawn round it so that passers-by can see and admire it.

'Where'll we put it in the flat?' she complains. 'We'll be on the seventh floor!'

Gwyn and Mary are being re-housed in a new block of flats which already towers above them a few hundred yards away. The building stands among pleasant gardens and from their living-room windows they will have a fine view of the River Thames.

'Why are they building all those skyscrapers?' asks Gwyn. 'Why don't they give us a council house that's got a garden back and front?'

'That's what I asked the man from the council this morning,' Mary replies. ' "Why don't you build more council houses?" I says. "We *are* building council houses," he says, "but if we build too many of them, London'll soon join up with Scotland!" "Very funny!" I says. "Well, you can laugh," he says, "but there's more room in the sky than on the ground. That's why we're building blocks of flats." "I don't want any of your flats," I says. "What!" he says. "You mean you'd rather stay in *this* place?" "What do you mean, 'place'! It's not a 'place'. It's our home. We came here the day we was married." '

'The rent will be higher in that new place,' says Gwyn.

'I won't like it, I know,' says Mary. 'Up on that seventh floor I'll never see anyone, except in the lifts, and they're always breaking down. Mrs Baker—you know, the one on the sixth floor—fell down the stairs yesterday with all her shopping. She had to go to the doctor, she did.'

Both Gwyn and Mary tend to dislike and resist change of any kind, especially Gwyn. He has little sympathy with modern young people and is inclined to be suspicious of foreigners, although he would help anyone who was in trouble.

Many middle-aged Conservatives have the same attitudes and prejudices as Gwyn, but he and Mary always vote for the Labour Party.

'The Conservatives are for the bosses,' says Gwyn. 'Of course they are! It's natural! Most of their money comes from big business.'

JIM WILLIAMS

Gwyn and Mary have two sons, but Jim and his brother Gareth have nothing in common. Jim left school as soon as he could, at sixteen, and is already earning £20 a week as a packer in the fish market. He is both jealous and scornful of Gareth—jealous because Gareth is cleverer than he, and scornful because, although Gareth is the elder, he is still at school and is not earning any money. Jim keeps himself to himself. He spends much of his time taking his motor-bike to pieces and putting it together again.

'He's in love with that bike!' says Gwyn. 'It's not natural. Why doesn't he get himself a girlfriend?'

'How do you know he hasn't got one?' asks Mary.

'He never tells me anything!' complains Gwyn. 'I'd like to know what he's doing—when he's not with his motor-bike!'

'Mrs Smith says she's seen him with Rob Milligan and his gang. It worries me.'

'That lot! They ought to be locked up. I'm not having him going about with them. I'll talk to him, I will!'

'It won't do any good. You know it won't.'

Jim is not actually a member of the Milligan gang and he has not yet taken part in any of the fights which disturb the neighbourhood. But he is bored, bored by his job and bored by the long hours when he is free. That is why he takes his motor-bike onto the motorway and tries to ride it at 100 m.p.h. (160 kms an hour.)

GARETH AND CHRISTINE

Gareth Williams is ambitious. He does not yet know what he wants to be, but he has been told by his teachers that he will certainly win a place at a university, probably Oxford or Cambridge. He is leaving school at the end of term and is now waiting for the examination results. He knows that if his results are good he will not have to worry about the cost

Jim, Gareth and Christine.

of going to university, because the local council will pay for everything.

Yet Gareth has problems which worry him deeply. He is not happy at home. For the last year he has had to do his scholarship work in a small dark room, surrounded by the oily parts of Jim's motor-bike and deafened by the noise of a transistor radio.

Gareth is fond of his father. Gwyn is pleased that one of his sons is going to have a better chance to get on in life than he had when he was young. Gwyn left school when he was fourteen[4] and is more concerned about conditions at the factory than about the subjects Gareth is studying; so the two of them have little to say to each other.

Gareth's relationship with his mother is far less happy. She thinks he is perfect, and he finds her love and her pride in him difficult to bear. She never leaves him alone.

'I've got a special dinner for you today, Garry!'—'Come and give your old Mum a kiss!'—'Isn't he good-looking, Gwyn? Just like his Dad used to be!'—'Aren't you clever, Garry, to know all those things!'

There are times when Gareth runs out of the house for fear of exploding and hurting his mother's feelings.

'You haven't shaved again this morning, Garry!'

'No, Mum. I'm going to grow a beard!'

Gareth intends to grow a beard when he leaves school, chiefly because he knows his mother doesn't want him to. It is his way of rebelling, the first step towards breaking ties with a home for which he feels little sympathy.

He usually makes his escape to his girlfriend, Christine. Christine is a typist in the office of a local store. She has long legs, long fair hair, and she laughs a great deal—she often laughs at Gareth when he is too serious. Both her parents are school teachers in a primary school in the East End, one of the poorest parts of London. She has no brothers or sisters, but she has an understanding with her parents which Gareth envies. Gareth and Christine spend long hours together in coffee bars, at discotheques or walking in the parks. They discuss many things, including their parents.

'There isn't so much a generation gap in this country as an education gap,' said Gareth. 'Take your parents! I can talk to *them* about my work and politics and things. It's impossible at home.'

'Why do you worry such a lot?' said Christine. 'Take your Mum and Dad as they are! After all, you don't talk about your work with me—or about politics, for that matter!'

THE MACDONALDS

The Macdonalds live in a north London suburb. Peggy travels to the City[1] each day by underground—a tiring journey that takes three-quarters of an hour. Ian is a clerk in a local bank. The Macdonalds married young and have seven-year-old twins, Douglas and Jane.

Peggy, a trained secretary, went back to work when the children were three. She has been with her boss, a City businessman, for two years, and is one of the thousands of married women in Britain doing a full-time job. Like many such women she has long been critical of the attitude of male employers towards women workers.

But at the end of 1975 new laws came into force[5]. Now Peggy must receive the same pay as men doing the same job. She must also have the same opportunities for promotion, or of being accepted for any job for which she is qualified. Employers who advertise jobs usually reserved for men (engineers, builders, lorry drivers etc.) must now word their advertisements 'man/woman wanted' or 'person wanted' (see p. 71). Otherwise they can be fined.

Peggy is able to work full-time only because Ian's mother lives with them. Mrs Macdonald helps with the housework and the care of the twins, and she has her own ideas as to how children should be brought

Ian is very proud of his garden, although Peggy wishes he would leave more room for the children to play.

17

up. Peggy, who believes in allowing her children plenty of freedom, sometimes has arguments about this with her mother-in-law.

Ian's good humour and good sense help to keep the family peace. Ian is too good-humoured, in Peggy's opinion. She wishes he was more ambitious, but Ian is quite content to work at the bank from nine till five, and has no desire to get the necessary qualifications to become a manager. He is, in fact, more interested in his garden than in his work. Like so many Englishmen he is out in his garden in all weathers and at all hours, even planting his seedlings by lamp light if necessary.

Peggy admires his garden, but she sometimes complains.

'I love your new red roses, Ian, but you've dug up so much of the lawn that there's no room left for the children. They're always going next door to play with the Painter children now.'

'Well, they can't do any harm there. Sid Painter's garden is a wilderness.'

Sid Painter's garden is the only one in Woodbury Avenue that is not neat and tidy and gay with flowers. The fences which separate the gardens are boundary lines and when Ian looks over them he sometimes makes envious or self-satisfied comparisons.

As Peggy and Ian are out all day during the week, it is usually Ian's mother who keeps them up-to-date about their neighbours' activities. She misses little of what is going on in the street.

'The Browns have just got a new car. Old Mrs Potter says it's a foreign car and it's very expensive. Mr Brown must be earning more money than you do, Ian! Oh, Peggy, do you know what? Mavis Pink didn't go to work this morning. A very smart young man in a sports car came and took her out. Who do you think it can be?'

The houses in Woodbury Avenue and in the neighbouring streets and districts are not by any means all alike, but they have a style which could be called typically suburban—because there are houses like them in every suburb of every town and city in Britain. This style is difficult to describe. In fact, it is really a mixture of styles, including at one extreme, very modern, low, box-like buildings with lots of glass, and at the other, imitations and variations of architecture of past centuries. The great majority of suburban houses are privately owned and were built by speculative builders (building companies looking for quick profits).

The houses in Woodbury Avenue are semi-detached, that is to say they are joined together in pairs, like Siamese twins. The semi-detached is one of the most characteristic houses of Britain, and is far more common in the suburbs or outskirts of a town than it is in the town centre, or in the country.

Strictly speaking, 'suburban' means 'on the edge of the city'. Suburbia is neither town nor country, but the word suburban has come to suggest something else. Like the French word, *bourgeois*, it now suggests a state of mind, an attitude towards life. Suburban people, like the French *bourgeoisie*, work in towns and are for the most part comfortably off. They are sometimes accused of being conservative, conventional, narrow-minded, unintellectual and snobbish; but if being typically suburban means all these things, then many people who live in the cities and in the country are probably typically suburban too.

There is, in fact, greater variety among the millions who live in suburbia than in any other part of Britain. People from every trade, business and profession live there, as well as large numbers of better-off working people, so their opinions and attitudes differ very widely indeed.

Take the Macdonalds' neighbour, Sid Painter, for example. He runs a small art magazine, grows his hair long, and helps alcoholics in his spare time. He is a member of the Communist Party. The Jacksons, who live on the other side of the Macdonalds, are extremely conventional. They continually complain about the noise which the twins make, and are shocked when Peggy sunbathes in her bikini.

Not surprisingly, most of Britain's floating voters come from suburbia. Floating voters are people who do not have any particular political loyalties: they 'float' between the parties instead of 'swimming' with one party. They usually do not make up their minds which party to support until the last minute, and it is often they who decide the results both at general and local elections.

'I don't think I'll vote at the next election,' said Peggy, after listening to a political talk on the radio. 'It won't make any difference to us which party gets in.'

'Everybody ought to vote,' said Ian.

'Well, if I do, I'll vote Labour. I think their ideas on education are better.'

Ian, who always votes Conservative, disagreed, but they did not quarrel. They rarely argue about politics.

Sir Eric is managing director of a large machine-tool company. He is about to retire, and is going to hand over the business to his son, Charles, next year. He is still a respected figure in the business world, even among the younger generation, who consider many of his views old-fashioned. Sir Eric himself sometimes finds it difficult to understand the younger generation and, after a few glasses of wine, he will admit this to his friends.

'I'm not as young as I was. I don't mix enough with young people. It's not easy when you live buried in the country, as I do.'

Sir Eric travels home every evening to his house in the country on trains crowded with thousands of other people who work in offices. Blakeney Hall is a large, seventeenth-century building standing in a park full of oak trees which are as old as the house. The park is surrounded by woods well stocked with pheasants, which Sir Eric and his friends enjoy shooting during the season. Yet, in spite of his liking for blood sports, Sir Eric has a real love of wild animals. He is an enthusiastic bird-watcher and is a member of the Wild Life Preservation Society. He is an open air man with few intellectual interests.

As one might expect, Sir Eric is a Conservative. His friends are Conservatives too—at least, it would never occur to Sir Eric that they weren't. He is proud of his country's past and sad, sometimes angry,

Sir Eric and Lady Blakeney outside their country home.

when ancient traditions disappear or are attacked.

He does not understand young people. They disturb and alarm him. His daughter, Susan, who is twelve years younger than Charles, is continually surprising and worrying him with her different sense of values and her different way of thinking.

'The young people of today don't seem to have any sense of responsibility,' he said to his wife, Hester. 'Take that long-haired boyfriend of Susan's—Jeremy something or other. Doesn't he have any pride? Doesn't he ever look at himself in the mirror? And who does he think he is, dragging Susan off to all those demonstrations?'

'Susan doesn't have to go with him if she doesn't want to.'

'When I was a student we didn't threaten the university authorities when we had a grievance. We didn't occupy university buildings and refuse to leave.'

'Perhaps not, but you did paint someone's statue red and have a fight with another college. You did get drunk after a college match, and get thrown out of a pub because you smashed all the bottles. I've heard you tell those stories many times—with pride.'

'That was different,' Sir Eric interrupted. 'Not the same thing at all. We weren't anarchists and we didn't take drugs. We respected authority, even if we didn't always like it.'

'Of course, dear,' Hester replied. 'But I don't think Jeremy is an anarchist and we've no reason to suppose that he takes drugs. From what I've heard he seems to be a very intelligent young man, which is probably why Susan likes him. I think we can trust her to choose her friends intelligently.'

'Well, I wish she lived at home, where we could keep an eye on her.'

LADY BLAKENEY

Hester Blakeney came from a less conventional background than Sir Eric. Her father was a London architect. She is not particularly intellectual, but she has wide interests, enjoys travelling abroad and has many friends not connected with the business world. She and Sir Eric lead independent lives for much of the time, but she entertains his business friends for him, and they go on holidays together. Although she is not particularly interested in politics, she does take part in the activities of the local Conservative Party, because she is Sir Eric's wife.

She takes part in their social or money-raising activities, but refuses to join any committees.

'They all get so serious when they sit on committees,' she told Susan one day, 'and I can't agree with everything they say or think. Very often it isn't *what* they say so much as *how* they say it. They're always so sure they're right! I had an argument with Phyllis Blandford about that last demonstration you took part in. Of course, we parted the best of friends, but I'm sure she thinks I'm a bit pink! (i.e. left-wing). As you know, I didn't really approve of the demonstration myself, but I wasn't going to tell *her* that!'

Hester tries to understand the point of view of young people, and she and Susan are good friends.

SUSAN BLAKENEY AND PENNY MARTIN

Susan is studying English at London University. She could, if she wished, live in her father's flat in the West End of London, which he hardly ever uses. Instead, she shares two rooms with a photographer's model, Penny Martin, in the less fashionable district of Pimlico. Susan gets an allowance from her father, but refuses to accept more than she would get from the local council as a university student. She takes no part in fashionable society life.

'If I had a father with all that money,' said Penny, 'I wouldn't refuse it!'

Penny is not a top-class model and never has enough money to buy all the clothes she would like. She is an orphan. Her mother died when she was fifteen and her father, a travelling salesman, was killed in a road accident. Her brother, Jeremy, is Susan's boyfriend, and that was how she and Susan came to live together.

Penny can't afford to buy the expensive clothes she models for magazines.

JEREMY MARTIN

Jeremy Martin, seen from behind, could be taken for a girl. His hair, a mass of tight curls, covers the back of his neck, and he likes to wear loose jackets and bright-coloured shirts. Jeremy went to university when he was eighteen and, at the age of twenty-one, got an excellent degree in history.

While at university Jeremy took an interest in university politics and was elected president of his students' union. Some of his activities were reported in the newspapers. He organised a successful four day sit-in in a dining-hall as a protest against the high prices charged for the very poor food. He led protest marches and demonstrations of all kinds. It was at a demonstration outside a foreign embassy that he first met Susan. For the past year he has had a variety of jobs in London, and at present is working in a second-hand bookshop in Charing Cross Road, near Leicester Square. He rents a small room in a poor district south of the river, and spends much of his spare time writing poetry and playing the guitar.

'You're a drop-out!' said Penny. 'You're just avoiding re-sponsibilities. Why don't you get a proper job?'

'I will, when I find one that suits me. But I'm damned if I'm going to put on a dark suit and work in an office from nine till five.'

'You wait, Jeremy!' said Penny. 'You'll want to make money like all the rest sooner or later. Then you'll put on a suit, cut your hair and say

"Yes, sir!" "No, sir!" to the boss!'

'I'll never do that!' said Jeremy. 'I don't want to be like everyone else.'

'Who do you want to be like, then?'

'I want to be me, and I want other people to admit that I've got a right to be different from them if I choose. That's why I'm so anti-Establishment[3]—because the Establishment thinks it's got a right to set our standards and decide our way of life. Without the Establishment there couldn't be any bourgeois materialism, and I hate that more than anything else. I hate it because it's the root of all our troubles, and I don't want to be part of it.'

'You *are* part of it—you and Susan. You go down to Blakeney Hall and enjoy the good food and wine there, don't you?'

'You're right, Penny,' said Susan. 'And this worries us, doesn't it, Jeremy?'

Susan and Jeremy have not yet voted, since neither of them has faith in any of the political parties. In fact, they have no confidence in government.

'Are you anarchists, then?' asked Penny. 'Are you suggesting that this bourgeois society, as you call it, should be overthrown by violence?'

'No, of course not! You know we hate violence,' said Susan. 'But there's so much misery and selfishness in the world, are you surprised we want to do something about it?'

'But *what* do you want to do?' insisted Penny. 'That's what you still haven't told me. The trouble with you, Sue, is that you're an idealist, but as for Jeremy—I think he's just a cynic!'

CHARLES BLAKENEY

'Can you stay on again this evening, Miss Gardener?' Charles said to his secretary one evening, 'I want to get these plans for the new factory off this week.'

'Well, my boyfriend won't like it, but—'

'Tell him about all that extra money you'll be earning!'

'I told him about that last time—and he wasn't very impressed! Don't you ever take an evening off yourself, Mr Blakeney?'

'Of course! But some things can't wait, can they?'

Charles Blakeney has just returned from Australia, where for three years he managed with great success the Melbourne branch of the firm.

He plans to make important changes in the business next year and his first job will be to improve the relationship between workers and management. Although Charles shares some of Sir Eric's views on the value of tradition, in practical business matters he is far more progressive. He believes in worker participation. In other words he believes that workers should have a share in making decisions which affect their working conditions. He likes to have discussions with representatives from the factory workshops and would not hesitate to choose an able worker for a post on the management side in preference to a less able man from his own background.

Unlike Sir Eric, who tends to be patronising, Charles gets on well with people from different backgrounds. However, he finds it difficult to get on with his sister's generation. He and Susan frequently disagree, about politics, about her own activities — and about making money!

'You're always talking about profits, Charles!'

'Rubbish!' said Charles. 'Anyway, it's impossible to carry on and improve a business unless it makes a profit. You seem to think there's something dishonourable about being in business.'

Charles' Australian wife, Anne, sometimes takes sides with Susan.

'Susan and her friends have got some interesting ideas. You're always criticising your father's generation. Why shouldn't she criticise yours?'

'There's only twelve years difference between Sue and me!'

'Be careful, Charles! People who make excuses like that are already on the way to middle age!'

HERBERT PERKINS

Herbert, the son of a textile worker in Manchester, left school at fourteen. After working for three years in an advertising office, he discovered that he had a gift for salesmanship. He was taken on by a firm making a rather poor quality soap powder, and went from door to door persuading housewives it was just what they needed. With the money he saved he bought a small shop in a busy street, painted it and stocked it with sweets. He had noticed that there were a lot of children in the neighbourhood, but no sweet shops. He was tough, ambitious and never afraid of saying what he thought.

After a few years, the sweet shop grew into a food store, and soon Herbert was buying shops in other parts of the city. Ten years later there were Perkins Stores all over the north.

When he was forty Herbert bought up a chain of supermarkets in the south, and moved to London with his family. He bought a house in a pleasant residential part of south-west London and found himself a neighbour of Charles and Anne Blakeney. Being hospitable and friendly, he at once asked the Blakeneys in for drinks.

'I hope you like it strong, Charlie!' he said, handing him a large whisky and soda. 'That's how we drink it up north!'

Herbert is glad to have Charles and Anne as neighbours because he recognises in Charles a businessman who, like himself, believes in hard work and profits. Herbert believes that everyone has the right to get rich, and the more money a man earns the more Herbert respects him. He has no patience with left-wing intellectuals or with some of today's young people who, he objects, 'expect to be fed with a spoon and are afraid of a bit of honest work and sweat'. Having made his own way in the world, Herbert disapproves of what he calls state interference; for example, he is against state aid to industry.

'Nobody helped me,' he says. 'If an industry is inefficient and can't pay its way, why should the state use tax-payers' money to help it?'

He also disagrees with Charles about worker participation. He himself does not hesitate to sack workers whom he considers to be lazy or inefficient—even at the risk of strikes—but, like Charles, he encourages those who work well by offering good wages and chances of quick promotion.

Elizabeth and Leonard Townsend in their modern kitchen.

'You and Anne are classy,' he said to Charles. 'But I don't give a damn for class, just character. I'm a northerner, lad!'

LEONARD AND ELIZABETH TOWNSEND

Leonard, the son of a Sheffield steel worker, went to the local grammar school (see p. 144) and from there won a scholarship to Oxford University. At Oxford he distinguished himself both as an actor and as a writer for the university magazine. He wrote critical articles about the university authorities, some of which were discussed in the national press.

After leaving university Leonard travelled all over the world, sending reports of his adventures to different magazines and newspapers. His gift for getting on with people earned him a job as a reporter at the BBC, and by the time he was thirty, he had become one of the BBC's youngest, most distinguished and — at times — most feared interviewers.

Leonard likes to think of himself as a 'liberal' — that is, somebody who is open-minded and unprejudiced. This is partly why his political sympathies are with the Liberal Party.

'The Liberal Party is the only one that doesn't think in terms of "class" all the time,' he said to his wife Elizabeth. 'The Liberals also dare to have new ideas on how to improve conditions in this country — which is more than you can say for the Conservatives or your precious Labour Party, Liz!'

'It's easy to have new ideas when you know you're never going to be asked to put them into practice,' said Elizabeth, who has little patience with the Liberals. She feels that most people who vote Liberal do so as a protest against the two main parties.

'You feel "safe" when you vote Liberal,' she often tells Leonard, 'because you know there are too few Liberal members of Parliament for them ever to form a government. In fact, you've got your feet firmly planted in mid-air!'

'If you think that,' Leonard replies, 'You just haven't bothered to find out what the Liberals stand for. The Liberals have often led the way for the other parties — going into the Common Market is just one example.'

Elizabeth is twenty-nine and a social worker in the East End of London. She has written a much talked-of book called *Children in Need*. Leonard first met her when he interviewed her in a television programme about children's playgrounds. Now, they have been married for three years and live in a small, early nineteenth-century house in north London. Elizabeth hopes to have a family one day, but does not intend to let it interfere with her work too much.

'We're lucky,' she said to Leonard. 'We could pay Alice to look after our children while I'm out at work. But most working-class mothers can't afford to pay anyone.'

'There are crèches (public nurseries), aren't there?'

'Yes, but there aren't enough. If the government really wants equality between men and women it'll have to provide crèches for the babies of *every* working mother.'

'Some mothers like to bring up their children themselves,' Leonard said.

Elizabeth and Leonard are both interested in literature, music, painting and the theatre. Leonard plays the piano well, reads widely and has a small but valuable collection of old English furniture. He and Elizabeth both take exercise by going for long country walks. Leonard has a strong prejudice against 'games-playing philistines'. By this he means people who are interested only in sport. They have a weekend cottage on a south coast estuary, where they keep a small and rather ancient sailing-boat.

NOTES

(1) *City*: The City (note the capital C) refers only to the oldest part of London, which is governed by the Lord Mayor of London (other parts of London each have their own mayor). The City is the business and commercial centre of London and includes the Bank of England, the Stock Exchange, the central Law Courts and St Paul's Cathedral.

(2) *Sir*: Sir Eric Blakeney, Bart. (short for baronet) belongs to the lowest rank of the nobility. He inherited his title from his father and will pass it on to his son. If there is no son, the title passes to the nearest male relative. *Knights* also have the title Sir, but they do not belong to the nobility and do not pass their title on to their sons. They receive their knighthoods as a reward for service to the nation. Politicians, scientists, businessmen, writers, musicians, actors and sportsmen have been knighted. The wife of a baronet or a knight is called Lady; for example, Lady Blakeney. If a woman is rewarded for services to the nation, she is given the title Dame (the equivalent of a knight); for example, Dame Peggy Ashcroft (a well-known British actress).

(3) *Establishment*: The Establishment is composed of those people, mostly older

people, who represent orthodox, conservative views and behaviour—in government, in education, in religion, in the arts and in society. It is a term largely used by people to the left (in the *not* strictly political sense of the word). But the Establishment is also criticised and made fun of by plenty of middle-class middle-aged people with moderate views.

(4) The school leaving age was raised from fourteen to fifteen in 1947, and to sixteen in 1974.

(5) *Women and work*: The Equal Pay Act, 1970, and the Sex Discrimination Act, 1975, came into force on December 29th, 1975.

QUESTIONS
(1) Mary Williams can see only the disadvantages of living on the seventh floor. Can you find any reasons why she should change her mind?
(2) Would you rather be earning money, like Jim, or studying like Gareth?
(3) Would you marry someone if you disagreed about politics?
(4) Would you be a 'floating voter'?
(5) What do you feel about equality for women? Are there any laws like this in your country?

FURTHER READING

Thomson, D.	England in the twentieth century
Sampson, A.	The New Anatomy of Britain Today (Hodder)
Jackson, B.	Working Class Community
Mitford, J.	Hons and Rebels (F)

The name 'the United Kingdom' is now used
for the political unit represented at the
United Nations. It was first used in
1801, when Great Britain and Ireland
were formally joined. 'Great Britain'
is an older name, which was
first used on the accession of James I
in 1603.

The British Isles — seen in
a wider geographical context.

James VI of Scotland, who
became James I of England.

Weather forecast and recordings

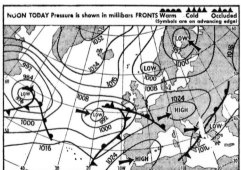

NOON TODAY Pressure is shown in millibars FRONTS Warm ●●●● Cold ▲▲▲▲ Occluded ▲●▲●
(Symbols are on advancing edge)

NOON TODAY

Today

Sun rises :   Sun sets :
7.21 am   4.10 pm
Moon sets :   Moon rises :
11.5 am   1.39 pm
Full Moon : November 20.
Lighting up : 4.40 pm to 6.52 am.
High Water : London Bridge. 8.16

variable for a time then W, strong ;
max temp 10°C (50°F).
E, NE and Central N England,
Borders : Mainly dry, mist or fog
patches at first, sunny periods but
rather cloudy at times ; wind variable becoming E, moderate or
fresh ; max temp 7°C (45°F).
W Midlands Wales : Mostly

Yesterday

London : Temp : max, 6 am to
6 pm, 9°C (48°F) ; min, 6 pm to
6 am, 2°C (36°F). Humid, 6 pm,
60 per cent. Rain, 24 hr to 6 pm,
none. Sun, 24 hr to 6 pm, 7.3 hr.
Bar, mean sea level, 6 pm, 1,021.6
millibars, steady.

2

The Mixture which is British

Britain, Great Britain, the United Kingdom (UK for short), England, the British Isles — these different names are sometimes used to mean the same thing, and they are frequently used wrongly.

The name used at the United Nations is the 'United Kingdom'; in full, this is the 'United Kingdom of Great Britain and Northern Ireland'. Strictly speaking, England, Great Britain and the British Isles ought only to be used as geographical names, since England is only a part of Great Britain; Great Britain does not include Northern Ireland, but the British Isles include Great Britain and the whole of Ireland, that is both Northern Ireland and the Republic of Eire.

There is a further confusion. British people ought really to be called Britons, but they seldom are. Instead they are most often called Englishmen. This annoys the Welsh, the Scots and the Irish, who dislike being called English, even if they live in England.

Gwyn Williams, for instance, would never call himself an Englishman, although he has lived and worked in London since he was fifteen. He was born in Cardiff and both his family name and his Christian name are Welsh.[9] He has not a drop of English blood in him.

Ian Macdonald, too, always thinks of himself as a Scot. Both Ian and Macdonald are Scottish names. Yet Ian has never lived in Scotland; his father and mother left their home town, Inverness, and settled in London as soon as they were married. Ian's wife Peggy — she was Peggy O'Flaherty before she married — is pure Irish. She was born of Catholic parents in Londonderry in Northern Ireland.

The English are Anglo-Saxon in origin, but the Welsh, the Scots and the Irish are not. They are Celts, descendants of the ancient people who had crossed over from Europe to the British Isles centuries before the Roman invasion. It was these people whom the Germanic Angles and Saxons conquered in the fifth and sixth centuries A.D.[5]

These Germanic conquerors gave England its name—'Angle' land. They were conquered in turn by the Norman French, when William of Normandy landed near Hastings in 1066. It was from the union of the Norman conquerors and the defeated Anglo-Saxons that the English people and the English language were born. Sir Eric claims that he is descended from one of William's knights. The Danes, or Vikings, who invaded Britain in the eighth century, also stamped their influence on the people and the language.

THE ENGLISH

Since 1066 the blood of many other races has been added to the original English mixture. Not only have Welsh, Scots and Irishmen made their homes in England, but also Jews, Russians, Germans—people from almost every country in Europe—as well as many West Indians, Indians, and others from the Commonwealth.[7]

As the English are such a mixed people, local customs and accents in England vary a great deal and local pride is still strong in some parts of the country. Both Leonard Townsend and Herbert Perkins always think of themselves as northerners, although they have moved to the south. Leonard is as proud of being a Yorkshireman as Ian Macdonald is of being a Scot.

The closer one gets to London, the less one notices such differences, for London is a melting-pot. People from all over Britain and from all over the world pour into the giant city. London tends to 'melt down' and smooth out strong accents and provincial customs. Every year the influence of London spreads further and further into the country, north, south, east and west, but particularly into the south and south-east. In an effort to stop London from spreading any more, new 'overspill' towns are being built forty to fifty miles outside London (see also Chapter 5, p. 94–97). London firms are encouraged to move to a new town, or at least to open new branches there instead of in another part of London. This policy is now beginning to have results. Until recently the greater

London region had a population of twelve million, but this figure is starting to drop.

The greater London region is roughly a circle, extending twenty to thirty miles from central London in the north and east, and thirty to forty miles in the west and south. Many of the old country cottages in the southern counties of Hampshire, Sussex and Kent have been turned into homes or weekend houses for well-off Londoners. Some people travel to work in London from as far as eighty miles away. Perhaps it is not surprising, therefore, that the Hampshire, Sussex and Kent accents are now rarely heard. Yet, strange to say, one of the strongest and most unusual accents is to be found in the East End of London, the home of the cockneys. A cockney is a Londoner who is born within the sound of Bow bells—the bells of the church of St Mary-le-Bow in east London. The cockney 'language' is really more than an accent, since it includes many words and expressions that cannot be heard in any other part of the country.[11] A cockney is very different from most people's idea of a typical Englishman. It is as difficult to find a typical Englishman as it is to find a typical Briton.

THE WELSH

Gwyn Williams' sons, like their mother, speak with cockney accents. They are complete Londoners but Gwyn himself has resisted being 'melted down' and 'smoothed out'. His Welsh accent is as strong as that of his brother who still lives in Cardiff.

Before they were conquered by the English in the thirteenth century, the different Welsh tribes were continually fighting one another. The conquest united them. Today, the small but passionate Welsh Nationalist Party (in Welsh 'Plaid Cymru') would like the Welsh to have their own parliament, instead of electing members to represent them in the United Kingdom parliament at Westminster, in London. Since 1959 there has been a Secretary of State for Wales. There have been Welsh ministers in the Cabinet and one of the most famous Prime Ministers of this century, Lloyd George, was a Welshman. In 1955 Cardiff was named the capital city of Wales. But this is not enough to satisfy many Welshmen. Although Plaid Cymru is still a small party, it won a seat at Westminster in 1966, two in February 1974 and three in October 1974.

'I don't see why Wales shouldn't have a parliament to look after Welsh affairs,' said Gareth, 'but Wales could never exist as a separate country. The Welsh need English money.'

'That's what your Uncle Owen says,' said Gwyn. 'But he doesn't like being told what to do by London.'

'Does Uncle Owen vote Welsh Nationalist?' asked Gareth.

'He says he's thought about it, but he still votes Labour,' answered Gwyn.

'If I lived in Wales, I'd join the Welsh National Army,' said Jim.

'You would,' said Gareth. 'You'd make a good terrorist!'

Very few Welshmen have any sympathy for the little band of patriots who call themselves the Welsh National Army. Plaid Cymru does not support this group which has done little more than blow up a few public buildings and the pipes carrying water from the lakes of central Wales to industrial cities in England.

Less than three million Welsh people live in Wales, although there are many others living and working in England and abroad. But a Welshman can usually be recognised by his accent, as well as by his name, even when he has lived most of his life away from Wales and cannot speak a word of Welsh. Today only about 25 per cent of the population can speak Welsh, and about 1 per cent (26,000 in all) speak *only* Welsh. In 1901 twice as many Welshmen could speak the language. Welsh is an ancient Celtic language, more different from English than English is from French or German.

In 1535 Welsh was forbidden as an official language, but in 1965 it was given equality with English for all official use in Wales. Nowadays some extreme nationalists demand that only Welsh should be used in the law courts in Wales, and on the road signs. To those who speak it, and even to those who do not, the Welsh language symbolises the whole of Welsh history and culture.

Gwyn Williams, like most Welshmen from the industrial cities and coal mining valleys of South Wales, speaks and understands only a very few words of Welsh. 'Mae hen wlad fy nhadan' (Land of my Fathers) he sings at rugby matches, but when—once every ten years—he visits his farming cousins in central Wales he does not feel at home.

'They say things about me in Welsh and laugh when I don't understand,' he complains. 'It makes me feel like a foreigner!'

The study of Welsh is now compulsory in primary and secondary schools in Wales, and television and radio services in Wales give about half their time to Welsh language programmes. However an all-Welsh broadcasting station which started in the 1960s did not last long because it had so little support from the people. The fact is that for many years the use of Welsh has been steadily growing less, in spite of all the efforts to strengthen Welsh national feeling by encouraging the language.

'But you ought to go to an international rugby match at Cardiff,' Gwyn tells his English friends, 'and listen to the crowd singing "Land of my Fathers". It puts the fear of God into the English team, I can tell you!' Rugby is the Welsh national game.

The Welsh are very musical, and many of their singers have become world famous. Every year a national festival is held. It is called the 'Eisteddfod' (Welsh for a 'sitting') and lasts several days. National costumes are worn, and competitions are held in Welsh poetry, music, singing and art.

Wales is divided geographically into the industrial south, the central plateaux and lakes, and the mountainous north of the farmers and tourists. About half the population is crowded into the south, where the coal mines are. Welsh coal is of very good quality and used to be exported all over the world.

'It was a great industry once,' Gwyn told his family. 'But you should have heard my Dad talk about it. Terrible conditions he had to work

The Welsh language is a powerful — and visible — symbol for the nationalists.

under, and very little pay. Men like my Dad never forgot or forgave the mine owners.'

The coal mining industry was nationalised in 1947. In the last few years the less productive coal mines have been closed down, but the crowded, ugly mining valleys of South Wales are still active, and the remaining mines have been modernised.

'There's good money in coal these days,' said Gwyn, 'now that oil is so expensive.'

'Yes! There's good money, because whenever the miners strike they get a rise,' Gareth said.

'And why not?' Gwyn said. 'They've never had a fair deal.'

'Fair deal?' Gareth cried. 'They're just about the richest workers in Britain!'

'Well, there's less chance of being out of work these days down the mines than at that steelworks they've put up at Port Talbot. Things have changed.'

The steelworks at Port Talbot is one of the biggest in Europe. During the mid-seventies the nationalised steel industry had a hard time. It was losing millions of pounds a week, and thousands of steel workers lost their jobs.

'Take your cousin Ifor,' said Gwyn. 'He left the mines for the steelworks and now he's lost his job there too. He says things are really hard in Wales.'

Wales lies on the edge of the United Kingdom. This semi-isolation helped to make the Welsh feel cut off and neglected. It also had serious effects on their industrial prosperity, for the main roads which led to their chief markets in England and Scotland were quite unsuited to heavy commercial traffic. Now motorways and a great suspension bridge across the River Severn link South Wales with all the most important cities in Britain.

North Wales is mountainous and has beautiful wild scenery. Its main industry today is tourism. It also attracts rock-climbers (see Chapter 14 Note 1). At the same time, the sheep-farmers of north and central Wales still carry on, with large flocks grazing on the lonely hills and moors and wandering across the unfenced roads. This is where you will certainly hear the Welsh language spoken.

But from whichever part of Wales they come, the Welsh are emotional, cheerful people, proud of their past, and welcoming to friends, but suspicious of 'foreigners', particularly the English.

THE SCOTS

The five million Scots have far more control over their own affairs than the Welsh.

'Why is the Scottish National Party necessary?' Peggy asked Ian. 'The Scots have their own system of law, their own church. They run their own education, housing and agriculture.' (For rapid growth of SNP see p. 86 Note 6.)

'The Scots don't dislike the English, Peggy. They just don't like being ruled from Westminster. They can't choose their own Secretary of State. This makes my brother, Duncan, mad. He says the English don't care a jot about Scotland. He says Scotland must have its own parliament, must decide its own economic policy, and must have its own representatives in Europe.'

'Duncan is an extremist.' Peggy said. 'He doesn't want to be part of Britain at all. He even wants a Scottish army! But it's North Sea oil that makes him really mad.'

'It makes most Scots mad! The oil fields are off the *Scottish* coast. Why should all the profits go to England?'

'They don't, Ian! They go to the country as a whole. Anyway, the Scots are doing pretty well out of the oil already—in every port up the east coast. And what about the oil off the Shetland Isles? The Shetlanders would rather belong to Norway than to Scotland.'

'Perhaps, but over half of all Scots now call themselves Scottish Nationalists.'

'And according to an opinion poll only 15% want complete independence! Do you want an independent Scotland, Ian?'

'If I lived in Scotland, I might. I admire the SNP leaders. They're intelligent. They know what they want and they're patriots. But I live in England, and I don't want to be a foreigner!'

Countless Scots have crossed the border and settled in England. Countless others, during the nineteenth century, settled in Australia, New Zealand, Canada and South Africa. The Scots were great empire-builders, and they were fierce soldiers, particularly the Highlanders. In World War I the Germans called them 'the Women of Hell' (because of their kilts).

In whatever part of the world a Scotsman lives, he usually knows whether his ancestors came from the Highlands or the Lowlands (see map p. 214). Highlanders usually consider themselves superior to Lowlanders. They argue that most Lowlanders are descendants of Anglo-Saxon settlers, and therefore not true Scots.

The few thousand Scots who live by the lonely lochs (or lakes) of the Western Highlands and on the windswept islands of the Hebrides, still speak Scottish Gaelic, an ancient Celtic language very like Irish Gaelic and related to Welsh. These Highland farmers, or crofters as they are called, lead a hard and simple life. They keep a few sheep and cows. They grow oats and potatoes, and they fish. Some have never seen a train or visited a city, although in the Orkney and Shetland Islands, islanders travel by plane more than most people in the UK. Many of the young people are moving south—attracted by the excitement and the greater opportunities of the cities.

Much of the Highlands is now owned by big landowners, many of whom are English or Lowland Scots. Some of these landowners have turned their land into great sheep or cattle farms, but many of them use their wild and beautiful mountain estates almost purely for pleasure— for shooting game or fishing for salmon.

The British government is trying to bring back life to the Highlands. One or two of the island communities now have modern fishing fleets. New industries and towns are growing up on the coast around Invergordon. Forests are being planted on the bare hills and saw mills and paper mills now stand on the edge of some of the lochs. New hotels

Aviemore—the centre of the Scottish tourist industry.

and roads are also being built, for the Highlands is one of the loveliest and least spoiled parts of Europe, in spite of the oil boom.

Tourism is one of Scotland's most important industries. Tourists from all over the world come to enjoy the beauty of Scottish scenery — to walk among Scottish heather, to visit ancient, historic castles, to eat Scottish salmon and to drink Scotch whisky (the word comes from the Gaelic 'uisge-(beatha)' — 'water (of life)'). They also come to see Scotsmen in kilts playing bagpipes, although only a few Scots wear kilts these days. The kilt is the national costume and every kilt has a squared coloured pattern, known as a tartan. The tartan means a great deal to a Scot, especially to a Highlander, for every Highland clan (Gaelic for tribe or

New hotels, like the one on the left, are essential to accommodate the great numbers of tourists.

Curling — a national game in Scotland for over 400 years. It is a team game played with heavy granite stones. The men are holding brushes; they sweep the ice to give the stone a smoother path to the target.

A rare sight except on ceremonial occasions, but an important symbol of the Scottish way of life.

family) has its own special tartan, of which it is jealously proud.

'Did you notice, Ian?' said Peggy one day. 'Emma Jackson is wearing a Macdonald tartan skirt with a scarf to match, and as far as I know she hasn't a drop of Scottish blood in her—not even Lowland blood!'

The Lowlands are densely populated and heavily industrialised. Cotton, iron, steel and coal are among Scotland's chief industries and the River Clyde, below Glasgow, is famous for its shipbuilding. It was here that the great Atlantic liner QE2 (Queen Elizabeth II) was built.

THE IRISH

Ireland was England's first colony, and this must never be forgotten when considering Irish history. Ever since the first English soldiers set foot on Irish soil eight centuries ago, there has been much misery and bloodshed.

Most people see the problem of Ireland as religious. Everyone agrees that the Irish people can be divided into two clearly cut religious groups, Catholics and Protestants. Everyone agrees that religious intolerance has helped to keep these two groups apart. But historians consider the problem of Ireland to be essentially colonial. The troubles of modern Ireland go back to the sixteenth and seventeenth centuries when, under the Tudor monarchs and later under Cromwell, English and Scottish Protestants were sent to Ulster as settlers. Their main duty was to keep a watch over the rebellious Catholic natives.

It is significant that the violence which broke out in Northern Ireland in 1969 began on August 12th. This is the day on which, every year, Protestants celebrate with marches and the beating of drums the defeat of the Catholic army which besieged them in Londonderry 200 years ago. Ulster Protestants celebrate other victories, particularly the Battle of the Boyne when, in 1690, William of Orange (William III of England) crushed the great Catholic revolution. These celebrations never fail to anger the Catholics.

At the end of the eighteenth century Protestant extremists formed a society which they called, in honour of William of Orange, the 'Orange Society'. The object of this society was to make sure that Protestant Loyalists (i.e. Protestants loyal to the British Crown) never lost control in Ulster. Orangemen throughout their history have always been militant. They have caused frequent riots, and they have fought Catholics at the slightest provocation. It was they who wrecked Lloyd

Londonderry August 1971.

George's plan for a unified Ireland in 1912. They armed themselves and threatened to fight rather than become part of the Catholic south.

It was Ulster Loyalists who forced the British government to partition Ireland. After a fierce and brutal war, the Irish were given their independence. In 1922, the Catholic south became an independent republic (Eire). But the Protestant north remained part of the United Kingdom. In Northern Ireland, or Ulster as it is often called, it was quite impossible to separate completely Catholics from Protestants. Whole Catholic communities were left behind—like islands in a Protestant sea. They became a minority, a large minority, since about a third of Ulster is Catholic. Few of these Catholics wanted to move to the south. They were getting better jobs and more money in the north. Yet they were not satisfied.

'Ever since partition,' said Peggy Macdonald, 'Protestants have been getting the best jobs and the best houses. Some bosses have even refused to employ Catholics. As for the voting system, it has always been completely unjust. In Londonderry Catholics outnumber Protestants two to one, but the city council has always been run by Protestants. And how many Catholics have there ever been in Parliament?'

Northern Ireland sends twelve representatives to the Parliament in Westminster[6], but unlike Scotland and Wales, it also had a parliament of its own, called 'Stormont'. Stormont had the right to deal with all home affairs without interference from Westminster. But ever since it

41

was founded in 1922, it was controlled by one party, the Ulster Unionists, who were all Protestants. Since they were always in power, the Unionists had complete control of the police, the Royal Ulster Constabulary. This disturbed, angered and sometimes frightened the Catholics. Until 1969 the RUC was the only police force in the United Kingdom to carry guns. During the riots of 1969, some policemen used their guns and several Catholics were killed. At the request of the British government the RUC were disarmed and British troops were sent out to Ulster to keep the peace. They were welcomed by the Catholics.

Moderate Catholics at this time were not demanding revolutionary changes in Stormont. They were demanding only their civil rights (i.e. equality with the Protestants in all branches of society). The leaders of the Civil Rights movement were non-violent, and they had the support of many moderate Protestants. They believed that they could persuade Stormont by peaceful demonstrations. They organised their marches before the serious riots began, and they were stoned and beaten up by Protestant extremists. It was these attacks on peaceful demonstrators that started the violent battles between Protestant and Catholic extremists. In one battle Protestants used guns and killed six people. British troops now took a tougher line but the Catholics soon accused them of taking sides with the Protestants.

Many people claim that the tougher attitude of the army was made unavoidable by the behaviour of the most extreme of all anti-Unionist organisations, the IRA (Irish Republican Army). The IRA's object has always been the unification of Ireland—not a union under the present Catholic government of Eire, but a union planned and run by the political organisation of the IRA itself. The IRA has a long record of violence. It has fought not only against the British, but also against the 'free' Irish of the south. In the 1920s it was declared unlawful by the Irish government. In 1939 it carried out bomb attacks in Britain, killing a number of people. During the second world war it formed an alliance with the Nazis, and it is now said to be largely Marxist. Until 1969 it had little support in Ulster.

It was the riots of 1969 which gave the IRA their chance. The bitter people of the Catholic ghettos of Belfast and Londonderry welcomed the IRA, and the IRA bombers and gunmen knew that they could hide in these ghettos without fear of being given away. The people of the ghettos accepted them as their champions. At the same time they were afraid of them. It was dangerous to have relations with the 'other side'. There were 'executions'. Two girls were tarred and feathered for going out with British soldiers. The IRA, although still unlawful in Eire, were able to operate from across the Border, for the Irish police did little to stop them, and many southern Irishmen regarded them as heroes.

When the terrorism began on a large scale in 1970 the IRA was split into two rival groups, the Official IRA and the Provisional IRA. However, the object of both groups was the breakdown of society, the removal of the British army, the starting of a civil war between Protestants and Catholics and the destruction of Stormont.

The methods of the Provisional IRA were brutal. They planted bombs in crowded shopping centres. They claimed that they always gave warning of their bomb attacks, but every week people were killed and hundreds horribly injured. The headlines in the newspapers counted the dead. They said little about the injured. Yet one girl who did not die in an IRA bomb attack lost both her legs, an arm and an eye.

The IRA also killed soldiers and policemen. They shot at them from moving cars or from roof tops. They even called at houses with guns hidden under their coats and shot the men down in front of their wives and children.

The Civil Rights leaders and the IRA were bitterly opposed to one another. But when in August 1971, the Stormont Prime Minister, Brian Faulkner, supported by the British government, introduced internment, *all* Catholics and 'freedom fighters' were united. 'After internment', one Civil Rights leader said, 'there can be no more moderates.' 'Internment' means, quite simply, arresting people suspected of being enemies of the state, and keeping them locked up without trial for as long as the government thinks fit. The men arrested were all suspected of belonging to, or helping, the IRA. Internment was an attempt by Stormont to control terrorism. It had the opposite effect. The bomb attacks became much more frequent and much more violent. Many Catholics, who until internment had been opposed to violence, now believed that violence was the only way. Civil Rights leaders declared that the only solution was for Stormont to go.

In the rest of Britain there was great argument about internment, many believing that it was undemocratic and dangerous.

'Internment is completely against the spirit of British justice,' said Peggy (see p. 119).

'But they're locking up murderers or would-be murderers!' said Ian.

'How do we know *who* they're locking up?' said Peggy. 'How would you like it if soldiers could knock on your door at any time of the day or night and take you off to a concentration camp? That's what internment means.'

'Why can't Catholics and Protestants in Ireland get on together — like you and me?' said Ian.

'A great many do,' said Peggy, 'but Protestants and Catholics have never lived together as one community in Northern Ireland, as they do here. So they've never had a chance of getting to understand one another. There wasn't a single Protestant family in our street in Londonderry, and there wasn't a single Protestant child in my school. My father worked with Protestants in a factory, but he wouldn't have dreamed of inviting one home. As far as I can remember none of us ever set foot in a Protestant house.'

Internment brought out the Civil Rights marchers again, and they marched in defiance of an order forbidding marches. On January 30th 1972, now called Bloody Sunday, paratroopers sent to stop a Civil Rights march, fired on demonstrators in the Catholic district of Londonderry. They killed thirteen people, none of whom was a known terrorist. Although the soldiers claimed that they had been fired on first, not one of them was either killed or wounded. After Bloody Sunday the Catholic Irish lost all confidence in the British government, and there was a hardening of attitudes everywhere.

A week later the IRA avenged Bloody Sunday by blowing up a building in the paratroops' headquarters in Aldershot, England. They killed six people but not a single soldier was seriously hurt.

In February 1972, a new Loyalist organisation called 'Vanguard' was formed by a former right-wing Stormont minister, William Craig. Its aim was to defend Stormont and keep the Ulster Protestants in control. It was violently opposed to direct rule from Westminster and yet wanted Ulster to remain part of the United Kingdom.

In an attempt to put an end to all the violence and misery, the British government took over full control of Northern Ireland, Stormont was suspended, at first for one year, and the Prime Minister and the cabinet resigned. An Englishman, William Whitelaw, was sent to Belfast as Secretary of State for Northern Ireland.

In 1973 representatives of the British and Irish (Eire) governments and the more moderate Protestant and Catholic leaders met at Sunningdale in England. They agreed to set up a power-sharing government of Protestants and Catholics in Northern Ireland. But the extremists on both sides refused to accept power-sharing. The Loyalists were particularly furious because they suspected that power-sharing would be the first step towards a United Ireland in which Protestants would be a minority. This is their constant fear.

In 1974 the Loyalist Workers Council called a general strike. This put an end to the power-sharing government and forced the British government to reintroduce direct rule from Westminster. Now militant Protestant groups showed that they could be as violent as the IRA.

In the same year IRA terrorists came to Britain, planting bombs in pubs, hotels, tube stations, anywhere where there were crowds of people. No warning was given and many people were killed or wounded, but by the end of 1975 the police had caught most of the bombers.

The gradual release of suspected terrorists from internment camps did not bring peace. Nor did the declaration of a cease-fire by the IRA late in 1974. The bitter opposition of the Loyalists to the idea of power-sharing with the Catholic minority made a solution impossible. So the bombings and killings went on. By 1976 hardly a day passed without Catholic killing Protestant, or Protestant killing Catholic.

In the summer of 1976 the Women's Peace Movement was founded. It was started by Betty Williams, a young Catholic housewife, after witnessing an accident in which a runaway IRA car crashed and killed two children and a mother. Betty Williams was so shocked that she decided to ask other women to join her in a fight for peace. She soon had thousands of followers, Protestants as well as Catholics. Almost at once they were threatened. They had stones thrown at them and members of their families were beaten up. But they had courage, and the Movement grew. They held big open-air meetings, they demonstrated and they marched, not only in Ulster, but in England, Scotland and overseas as well. They called for an end to violence from *all* sides.

IMMIGRANTS[8]

Foreigners have been settling in Britain since the beginning of the century. The number of immigrants was controlled, except for Commonwealth citizens, who, until 1962, were allowed to enter freely.

Before the second world war most of the immigrants came from the old dominions; Canada, Australia, New Zealand, South Africa. Then in 1952 a flood of immigrants started pouring in from the West Indies, India and Pakistant. They were poor and out of work and had been told there were jobs for them in Britain.

Coloured people soon became a familiar sight in every city. Nearly half the doctors in the National Health Service are coloured. Many nurses in N.H.S. hospitals are coloured, and large numbers of bus drivers and conductors are also coloured. But coloured immigrants have not had an easy time. Most of them have had to take the lowest paid jobs, and when there is unemployment they are usually the first to be sacked. In spite of laws to protect them, there is still discrimination by employers, by landladies and by club owners. Young West Indians who were born in England and are English in every respect except their colour, are especially bitter.

Britain's racial problems are often discussed on radio and television. Leonard Townsend has led many such discussions.

● LEONARD: I have with me four people who are concerned with race relations in Britain. On my right, Mr Jack Holder, secretary of a West Indian Association in west London; Mr Singh, born in

A multi-racial school with a multi-racial staff — small children have no colour prejudice.

Mr Enoch Powell was expelled from the Shadow Cabinet because of his speeches on immigration. (See Note 8.)

Calcutta, India, now a doctor in a big Bristol hospital; and Mrs Dawkins, headmistress of a primary school in Bradford, Yorkshire. On my left I have Mr Samuel Todd, who supports Mr Enoch Powell's views on immigration. Mr Todd, you claim that Mr Powell is — I repeat your actual words — 'only saying what every Englishman thinks'. Isn't that a slight overstatement?

MR TODD: Not judging from the letters I receive.

LEONARD: Isn't it rather strange, then, that according to an opinion poll held after the passing of the 1968 Race Relations Bill very few people expressed the strong feelings that Mr Powell claims are typical?

MR TODD: I think there can be no doubt at all that many people from all classes support Mr Powell. You may remember that not long ago London dockers marched to the House of Commons to demonstrate in favour of Mr Powell — even though they were Labour supporters.

LEONARD: What are your feelings, Mrs Dawkins? Do you feel that Mr Powell has a case?

MRS DAWKINS: Certainly not. If I remember correctly *The Times* used the adjective 'evil' to describe Mr Powell's first important speech on immigration. Another influential paper called it 'dangerous nonsense'. Not one newspaper with either Labour or Conservative sympathies had a good word to say for it.

47

LEONARD: Mr Holder, you left Jamaica fifteen years ago and are now a bus driver in London. What are your feelings about race relations in Britain?

MR HOLDER: Like everyone else, I'm worried. Racialism is a force all over the world, and not only between black and white. It is a force in Britain too. But it is not yet deeply rooted here. That is why, like Mrs Dawkins, I regret Mr Powell's speeches. His speeches encourage racialism, particularly among uneducated people.

LEONARD: Have you yourself suffered as a result of your colour?

MR HOLDER: Yes. When I first arrived in Britain I found it difficult to get lodgings. Landladies were quite polite to me, but they always found excuses for turning me away. I believe they were afraid of what the neighbours would think. I also feel that if it were not for my colour I would have a more interesting job now. It's an unfortunate fact that, at the moment, the more skilled a coloured man is, and the better he speaks English, the less chance he has of getting the job he wants.

LEONARD: Do you think that the setting up of the Race Relations Board was a good idea?

MR HOLDER: Undoubtedly. I don't think that things will be so difficult for my children as they have been for me.

MRS DAWKINS: I'm sure Mr Holder is right. Young children do not usually have colour prejudices. If they do, it's likely to be their parents' fault. I find that in my school West Indians, Pakistanis and white children all play happily together. Many coloured children have already grown up with cockney, Yorkshire or midland accents. They are exactly like English men and women in every respect except their colour. In fact, they *are* English men and women.

MR TODD: I cannot agree with Mrs Dawkins. They will always remain West Indians and Pakistanis.

MRS DAWKINS: Have you forgotten, Mr Todd, the large numbers of European immigrants who have settled in Britain? They didn't all receive a very warm welcome, I can tell you! In fact I wouldn't like to repeat some of the things that were said about them! But now they and their children—and grandchildren—are just like any other British citizens.

LEONARD: You, Mr Singh, have an important position in a big hospital. You clearly haven't suffered in the same way as Mr Holder. Why?

MR SINGH: Because everyone knows that the British Health Service would be in serious difficulties if it lost its Indian doctors and its West Indian nurses. There is an important lesson to be learned here. Coloured doctors and nurses are respected because of their professions. What I mean is, the proportion of coloured people in unskilled jobs is too large. There ought to be coloured people in positions of authority in *every* profession and trade.

MRS DAWKINS: I completely agree with Mr Singh. The English tend to be suspicious of foreigners. But they judge people by their jobs rather than by their race or nationality, don't you think? I'm thinking of the West Indians, Indians and Pakistanis who play in English cricket teams. They're the heroes of thousands of English sports lovers. And what about all the coloured musicians, entertainers and writers? We all admire and respect them, surely, without a thought for their colour. If we had a few coloured judges, not to mention more coloured headmasters and headmistresses—and more coloured bus inspectors—then I think you'd find the prejudices would soon go! After all, not so long ago many upper-class people would have been shocked to think that a man from a working-class background could ever rise to be prime minister.

LEONARD: Integration, living together as one community, is clearly the aim and wish of the great majority of English people. Mr Holder, how do you think that this integration can be carried into effect?

MR HOLDER: The biggest problem of all is the ghetto, the crowding together of large racial groups into one part of a city—very often the poorest and least attractive part of the city. This ought never to have been allowed. It was bad planning on the part of the authorities in the early stages of large-scale immigration. It was also partly the fault of the immigrants themselves, who felt frightened and lonely in a strange country and therefore *wanted* to remain together. People who live in separate communities are always regarded with suspicion, and sometimes even with fear.

LEONARD: Correct me if I'm wrong, but isn't it true that in some cities about a quarter of the population is now coloured?

MR SINGH: It is said that Bradford is the second largest Pakistani city in the world! Am I right, Mrs Dawkins? But I would like to add to what Mr Holder has just said. There is another problem—the problem of language. West Indians speak English, and although it isn't exactly 'standard' English, it is as much their language as it is a

Yorkshireman's or a cockney's. Therefore they have an advantage over Indians and Pakistanis. Many Pakistanis can't speak any English at all when they arrive in Britain.

MR TODD: Don't you agree, then, that in schools where there are large numbers of immigrant children who can't speak English, English parents are justified in complaining that the children are held back?

MRS DAWKINS: Yes. But this problem isn't nearly as serious as some people imagine. Many schools have special language classes for immigrant children who can't speak English.

LEONARD: Is it true that in some districts the authorities are encouraging integration by taking coloured children by bus to schools in white districts?

MR HOLDER: Yes. But this isn't a very satisfactory solution. The coloured children make friends with white children at school but live too far away to carry on these friendships when they get home. Provided that *all* schools get the same fair treatment from the authorities and that *all* children, whatever their race, colour, religion or class, get equal opportunities, it oughtn't to matter if a school is 75 per cent white or 75 per cent coloured.

MR TODD: I would remind you all of what is happening in the United States. Aren't we all burying our heads in the sand?

LEONARD: Wouldn't you admit, Mr Todd, that the conditions over here are a little different? Mr Powell suggests that Britain may one day be flooded with coloured people. He sees all kinds of dangers in this. But isn't he being unnecessarily alarmist? I have here some figures. It would seem that, even allowing for their present growth rate, the proportion of coloured people in Britain is never likely to top the 4 per cent mark.

MR HOLDER: And of that 4 per cent, Mr Todd, only a very small proportion indeed would ever consider using violence. Crime among coloured people is below the national average. We're not a violent people, Mr Todd.

MR TODD: But there's another point, surely? The English are going to lose their national characteristics—we won't be the same people any more!

MRS DAWKINS: Oh really, Mr Todd! How can you talk such nonsense! What are the English, anyway? We started as a mixture and a bit more mixture would probably do us more good than harm! In any event, as a genuinely multi-racial society we would be able to understand and help with other people's problems. With the world growing smaller each day, our only hope is to be able to live together with understanding and sympathy.

LEONARD: May I ask you all one last question? Are you hopeful about the future?

MR TODD: Not if present policies are continued.

MR HOLDER: I think there will be a long period of difficulty, misunderstanding, and even bitterness where there are ghettos. But yes, on the whole, I am hopeful. As Mrs Dawkins said, other foreign immigrants have been integrated—in the end. It may take longer with us, because our colour is a continual reminder that we're different. Then, with Pakistanis and Indians, there are the problems of religion, dress and eating habits. This makes integration for them more difficult still.

MR SINGH: The government must provide better housing, better education, and better opportunities for good jobs. If the government deals effectively with these essentials I think that integration will come sooner than many people think. For example, we have no colour problem in Bristol.

MRS DAWKINS: Exactly! We tend to forget the many places, like Bristol, where there is no bad feeling between the races. We're always hearing about the trouble spots. I sincerely believe that our grandchildren will wonder what we meant by 'colour problem'. If Mr Todd will excuse me, I cannot believe that Powellism will ever get a firm hold on the majority of decent English people.

NOTES

(1) Population of

UK (1971)		55,515,000
England		46,019,000
Wales		2,731,000
Scotland		5,229,000
N. Ireland		1,536,000

(2) Population of major cities (1971) and urban agglomerations (i.e. where two or more cities and their suburbs form a continuous built-up area).

City		Urban Agglomeration
London (the City)	4,245	
Greater London	7,452,000	

City		Urban Agglomeration
Birmingham	1,015,000	2,372,000
Glasgow	897,000	1,728,000
Liverpool	610,000	1,267,000
Manchester	544,000	
Sheffield	520,000	
Leeds	496,000	1,728,000
Edinburgh	454,000	

(3) Population density (number of people per square kilometre) (1973):

UK	229
England and Wales	325
Scotland	66
N. Ireland	109

Countries with higher population densities than the UK:

Netherlands	329
Belgium	320
Japan	291
West Germany	249

(4) Population growth rate (yearly rate of increase):

	1963–69	1970–73
World	1·9%	2·1%
Europe	0·8%	0·7%
UK	0·6%	0·3%
Africa	2·5%	2·8%
Latin America	2·9%	2·9%
North America	1·2%	1·3%
Asia (excluding USSR)	2·1%	2·3%
Oceania	2·0%	2·2%

(5) *How the Mixture was Formed*

55 B.C.	Romans under Julius Caesar invade Britain.
A.D. 410	Romans leave Britain.
450–600	Angles and Saxons conquer Britain, except for Cornwall (in the south west), Wales and Scotland.
793–978	Invasions by Danes (or 'Vikings').
1066	Normans, under William the Conqueror, invade and conquer the English at the Battle of Hastings.

Wales

1285	After 200 years of bitter fighting Welsh lose independence. But frequent wars and rebellions against English continue into the fifteenth century.

1535   Act of Union between Wales and England.

Scotland

Angles and Saxons invade and settle in Scottish Lowlands.

1200–1400   English try to conquer Scotland.

1314   English defeated at Battle of Bannockburn. From then on Scotland completely independent.

1603   Queen Elizabeth I of England dies childless. Nearest relation, James VI of Scotland, becomes James I of England, but full political union does not come for another 100 years.

1707   Act of Union. England, Scotland and Wales become Great Britain. Scotland loses her parliament.

1745   Failure of Jacobite rising under 'Bonnie Prince Charlie'. English take terrible revenge on Highlanders.

Ireland

1169   Anglo-Norman conquest of Ireland begins. Frequent and fierce rebellions from now on.

Early seventeenth century: English and Scottish Protestants sent by King to settle among Catholics in Northern Ireland.

1641   Great Irish Rebellion.

1649   Cromwell crushes rebellion. Thousands of Catholics killed by his Protestant soldiers. Further Protestant settlers sent to Northern Ireland.

1688   Irish rebel again.

1690   Rebellion crushed by William III at Battle of the Boyne.

1800   Act of Union.

1846   Potato famine—one million die of hunger. During second half of nineteenth century mass emigration to colonies and America.

1916   Rebellion in Dublin crushed by English.

1919   Irish Republic set up by Irish.

1920   Fierce fighting between English and Irish. Protestants of Northern Ireland support English.

1921–2   Ireland divided by agreement into Irish Free State (later Eire) and Northern Ireland (Ulster). Protestants of Ulster chose union with Britain. Britain now officially known as United Kingdom of Great Britain and Northern Ireland.

1949   Eire leaves Commonwealth. Took no part in second world war.

1968   Civil Rights Movement in Ulster: moderate Catholics, supported by some Protestants demand equal citizenship for all.

1969   Serious fighting breaks out in Londonderry and Belfast between Catholics and Protestants. Many houses burned, many people hurt, a few deaths. British troops sent to keep the peace.

1971   Internment of suspected terrorists.

1972   Direct rule from Westminster. Stormont suspended for one year.

1973
March   The 'Border Poll'. 60% of the electorate voted and decided by a very large majority to remain part of the UK.

May   Election of an Assembly of 78 members, with power to make laws.

December   Meeting at Sunningdale, England. It was agreed to set up a power-sharing government. The Assembly approved these proposals.

1974
January   Direct rule ended when the British government handed over certain powers to the Assembly. A Protestant (Faulkner) became leader of the new government with a Catholic (Fitt) as his deputy.

February   UK election: 11 out of 12 Northern Ireland constituencies elected MPs who were against power-sharing.
Merlyn Rees became Secretary of State for Northern Ireland.

April   The 3 main Loyalist parties joined together in the United Ulster Unionist Coalition and demanded the abolition of the Executive. 1000th victim of troubles died.

May   General strike called against the Sunningdale proposals. Faulkner resigned, the Assembly was suspended and direct rule from Westminster was reimposed.

1975
May   Convention elected to work out a new constitution. The Loyalists refused to accept the principle of power-sharing and the Convention ended its discussions in November.

1976
February   Merlyn Rees recalled the Convention in an attempt to produce a system of government acceptable to all. The parties in the Convention were still unable to reach agreement. The Loyalists continued to oppose the idea of sharing power with the Catholic minority.

July   British ambassador to Eire assassinated by IRA in Dublin.

(6) *Irish M.P.s at Westminster*
There are 12 Irish members at Westminster. In 1964 they were all Unionists, in 1966 the number of Unionists was 11, in 1970, 8. After the February 1974 election, there were 11 Unionist MPs. After the October 1974 election there were 10.

(7) *Commonwealth immigrants*: There are about one million Commonwealth immigrants living in Britain today. The figures given here are based on the 1971 sample census.

Commonwealth immigrants		*Foreign immigrants* (census 1971)	
Place of origin		*Place of origin*	
Africa	164,205	Republic of Ireland	720,000

54

Commonwealth immigrants		Foreign immigrants	(census 1971)
West Indies	304,070	Germany	157,680
India	321,995	Poland	110,925
Pakistan	139,935	Italy	108,980
Canada	64,665	Spain	49,470
Australia	57,000	France	35,910
New Zealand	21,155	USA	110,590
Cyprus	73,295	USSR	48,095
Sri Lanka	17,040		
Singapore	27,335		
Hong Kong	29,520		

Balance of migration: Many people fear that immigration will increase the population density, especially of England. Figures do not show that this is likely to happen. Between 1964 and 1968, one million people left the UK, as against one million who came in.

1974	Number leaving UK	—	269,000
	Number entering UK	—	183,800

(8) *Immigration*

By the early 1960s the numbers of immigrants coming to Britain were growing so large that it was obvious that action had to be taken to prevent overcrowding and unemployment. Since 1962 two kinds of action have been taken: the first, to reduce the numbers of new immigrants; the second, to protect people's rights, especially those of coloured immigrants.

a) *Reduction of numbers*

1962   The Conservative government passed the first Commonwealth Immigrants Act. Under this act the number of Commonwealth citizens who could come to Britain to live was limited to 8,500 a year. No control over citizens of the Irish Republic was introduced.

1965   The Labour government reduced the number of entries by half. It also refused entry to Britain to unskilled workers who did not have a job waiting for them.

1968   The Labour government passed the second Commonwealth Immigrants Act. This extended control to many who were counted as British citizens because they held passports issued by UK High Commissions abroad e.g. Asians in East Africa. Only a limited number of such citizens was allowed entry in any one year.

1971   The Conservative government introduced a bill which would treat Commonwealth citizens in the same way as other foreigners. The former would be given an entry certificate for a limited period if a job had already been arranged. The only people with an uncontrolled right to come and live permanently in Britain would be those born in the country, or those with at least one parent who was born in Britain.

None of these controls affected students coming to British universities, or people coming on training courses, or people visiting Britain for limited periods.

b) *Protection of Rights*

1965   The Labour government passed the first Race Relations Act. This act made it a criminal offence to stir up hatred on grounds of race. Between 1965 and 1970 there were sixteen prosecutions under this act and three people were sent to prison. At the same time a Race Relations Board was set up to look into complaints of racial discrimination.

1968   The Labour government passed the second Race Relations Act. Its main purpose is to make clear what discrimination means and when people have the right to go to the Race Relations Board. For example, the Race Relations Board can take action to prevent discrimination in looking for a house, lodgings or a job. On the other hand discrimination is not an offence if, for example, an employer employs less than ten people, or if he already has a racial balance among his employees which he wishes to keep.

1968   A Community Relations Commission (CRC) was set up. Its purpose is to advise the government, and to provide training in community relations work. Since 1968 local CRCs have been set up in many districts with the support of the local authorities. They advise local teachers, youth leaders, the police, and so on. There has been a great deal of criticism of these laws. Some people believe they are unfair, others that they have not gone far enough.

Race Relations Act 1968   Ch. **71**   1

ELIZABETH II

1968 CHAPTER 71

An Act to make fresh provision with respect to discrimination on racial grounds, and to make provision with respect to relations between people of different racial origins.   [25th October 1968]

BE IT ENACTED by the Queen's most Excellent Majesty, by and with the advice and consent of the Lords Spiritual and Temporal, and Commons, in this present Parliament assembled, and by the authority of the same, as follows:—

PART I

DISCRIMINATION

General

1.—(1) For the purposes of this Act a person discriminates against another if on the ground of colour, race or ethnic or national origins he treats that other, in any situation to which section 2, 3, 4 or 5 below applies, less favourably than he treats or would treat other persons, and in this Act references to discrimination are references to discrimination on any of those grounds.   *Meaning of " discriminate ".*

(2) It is hereby declared that for those purposes segregating a person from other persons on any of those grounds is treating him less favourably than they are treated.

Unlawful discrimination

2.—(1) It shall be unlawful for any person concerned with the provision to the public or a section of the public (whether on payment or otherwise) of any goods, facilities or services to discriminate against any person seeking to obtain or use those   *Provision of goods, facilities and services.*

The first page of the Race Relations Act of 1968.

The best known critic of Britain's immigration policy is a former Conservative minister, Enoch Powell. He demands an end to all coloured immigration and proposes that immigrants who are already here should be 'encouraged' to go home.

In 1968 Mr Powell made an anti-immigration speech which was so racialist in tone that the Conservative leader, Mr Heath, dismissed him from his position in the Party. Since that time, Mr Powell has made similar speeches in various parts of the country. In February 1974 he refused to stand as a Conservative at the election because he disagreed with his party over the Common Market (see Chapter 15). In fact he encouraged his followers to vote for the Labour Party, which at that time opposed the Common Market. In the October 1974 election, he stood as a Northern Ireland Unionist candidate and won the seat.

(9) *Family Names*
Scottish
Names beginning with Mac or Mc (*mac* is the Gaelic for 'son of'), e.g. MacGregor, McFarlane. Also, Fraser, Stewart (or Stuart), Campbell.
Irish
All names beginning with O, e.g. O'Henry, O'Flaherty. Also, many names beginning with Mul, e.g. Mulligan, Mulcahy. There are many names beginning with Mac, e.g. MacNamee, since the Irish language is also Gaelic.
Welsh
Jones, Williams, Thomas, Edwards, Owen, Lloyd, Llewellyn (many Welsh words begin with the Celtic ll).
English people often call Scots 'Jock' or 'Mac'; Welshmen, 'Taffy'; and Irishmen 'Paddy' or 'Mick'.

An eighth-century copy of an Anglo-Saxon manuscript by Bede.

57

(10) *Accents*

As in other countries, there are a number of different regional accents in the United Kingdom. Apart from Scottish, Welsh and Irish accents, the north, east, west and south-west of England, as well as the midlands and London, all have their distinctive accents. At the same time there is an accent which belongs to no particular region. This accent is called the Standard English accent, and is the accent usually taught to foreigners. Northerners call it the 'southern accent'— with some scorn. Some upper class people have an extreme form of this accent. An American would recognise this accent as English (or British) just as an Englishman would recognise a Scottish, American or Australian accent. But English people today, particularly the younger generation, are not nearly so conscious of accents as they were before the war. There used to be a kind of accent snobbery. This has almost disappeared.

(11) *Some examples of English Pronunciation*

North Country people pronounce 'come', 'up', 'love', etc., 'coom', 'oop', 'loov', etc. Cockneys do not pronounce their 'h's, e.g. 'house' is pronounced 'ouse', 'here', 'ere'. They pronounce 'plate', 'late', etc., as 'plite', 'lite', etc.

QUESTIONS

(1) Do you think that integrating people of different races *need* be a problem? Will it be a problem in twenty years' time?

(2) What is your feeling about nationalist parties?

(3) If you lived in the remote Scottish Highlands what aspects of modern civilisation would you miss most?

(4) In England we depend a great deal on immigrants for basic public services like transport and the health service. Are there other countries where this is true?

(5) In your view, is language an important factor in the problem of race relations?

FURTHER READING

Hepple, R.	Race, jobs and the law in Britain
Sunday Times Insight Team	Ulster
Rogers, J.	Foreign places, foreign faces *(Connexions)*
McInnes, C.	City of Spades (McGibbon) (**F**)
Mikes, G.	How to be an Alien

3

How the British Behave

THE POP REVOLUTION

'Pop' is short for popular, and popular, in its true sense, means 'of or for the people'.

The Pop Revolution of the 1960s (see p. 204) changed the pattern of English life. It gave the young an importance and influence they had never had before. Just how far-reaching that influence is, can be judged from a look at advertisements. The young are now regarded as one of the most important markets for consumer goods.

The Pop Revolution has broken down social barriers among the young. It has also helped to sweep away many of the inhibitions which gave the British their reputation for being cold and reserved. It was in the 1960s that people in Britain began to talk about the 'permissive society' and the 'generation gap'.

'The teenage girls who screamed hysterically over the Beatles,' said Elizabeth to Leonard one day, 'and the teenage boys who copied the Beatles and grew their hair long and were no longer ashamed of wearing "pretty" clothes, were simply breaking through traditional British reserve and fear of showing their feelings. I'm sure one of the main reasons why boys and girls are such good companions today is because they're no longer afraid of showing their feelings towards one another. A lot of the older people who criticise them are probably just jealous because they couldn't—or didn't—behave in the same way when they were young!'

A queue for a garden party at Buckingham Palace —and an onlooker.

150,000 fans at an open air pop festival in Somerset.

THE PERMISSIVE SOCIETY[1]

'Of course we ought to be permitted to think, speak and feel as we like,' said Jeremy, 'provided we don't do any harm to anyone else.'

'How do you know when you're doing harm or not?' said Penny. 'Would you permit people to take drugs, for example?'

'That depends on the drugs. Some of them can be harmful in all sorts of ways — like too much drink, and smoking as many cigarettes as you do, Penny!'

'Do you think that people should be protected against themselves, then?' asked Susan.

'Yes, I do, but I don't know how. I certainly don't believe we should be afraid of a really free society just because a few people wouldn't use their freedom sensibly. If you want to be free, you have to take a few chances.'

'What do your father and mother think about the permissive society, Sue?' asked Penny.

'Mother argues that it's far worse to be permissive about drunken drivers, whatever their age, than about students who block the roads with their demonstrations. Father only uses the word when he's thinking of young people. He's always talking about discipline and law and order, and how he would never have dreamed of talking to his father as I sometimes talk to him.'

'What really makes me mad' said Jeremy, 'is the attitude towards morals. Some people are really shocked because actors are allowed to walk about the stage without any clothes on these days, and they think it's right that the police should be able to walk into art galleries and decide whether pictures are works of art — or obscene. But these same people aren't shocked by advertisements which persuade the public to buy things which can do real harm — like cigarettes and alcohol, for example. I think a lot of advertisements are much more immoral than so-called pornographic, or "dirty", plays and books, because they lie — or at least disguise the truth.'

'How do you know that pornographic pictures and books don't do harm?' asked Penny.

'I didn't say they did no harm. I'm just suggesting that the whole question of morality is relative. I think the behaviour of some businessmen is relatively more immoral than that of some of the young people they criticise.'

'You seem to think that everything will be all right if you just allow people to be natural. Well, it's just as natural to want to cheat somebody as it is to want to run about the beach naked. I personally feel we all need some kind of outside authority to help us discipline ourselves.'

THE GENERATION GAP

Twelve o'clock drinks at Charles Blakeney's house[5]. Charles, Anne, Susan and Herbert Perkins are there.

HERBERT: I was young once myself, you know. I know what it's like to be young.

SUSAN: But you don't know what it's like to grow up in *our* world, Mr Perkins.

HERBERT: I grew up during the war, young lady.

SUSAN: Exactly! *You* had a brave new world to fight for, didn't you? But what have *we* got to look forward to? Pollution and the population explosion—if we're not destroyed first by the H bomb!

CHARLES: We'll survive, like all the generations before us. Progress is just moving a little bit faster, that's all.

ANNE: Really, Charles! Progress, as you call it, can change things completely in a few years these days. You know that perfectly well. Can't you understand how pointless your business world must seem to young people like Susan?

HERBERT: We have to go on living, Anne, and living means working. The young will realise that one day. They'll learn. They'll grow up.

SUSAN: You think we should grow up to be like you, don't you, Mr Perkins? I know Charles does. He laughs at us when we talk about universal love and understanding between people! When people demonstrate about what is happening in other countries, he says, 'What right have they to interfere? It's none of their business!' But it *is* our business, Charles. We're all responsible for one another these days, whatever our race or colour or nationality.

CHARLES: I agree, Sue, but so many of your so-called international demonstrations only make misunderstandings worse. A lot of you are so sure you've got the answer to everything. You won't accept any guidance at all from older people.

ANNE: But Charles, it's very difficult for older people to give proper guidance when, as Susan says, they've had no experience of being young *today*. It's no use their saying, 'I never behaved like that when I

62

was young'. They didn't have the same kind of problems. That's what the generation gap is all about.

CHARLES: Well, I don't think the generation gap in this country is as great as Susan makes out. In fact, I suspect she goes to her mother for advice just as often as she goes to friends of her own age!

HERBERT: We're always hearing about the old 'uns not understanding the young 'uns. What about the young 'uns understanding us? They don't try much, I must say!

SUSAN: You know, Anne, I'm almost frightened of getting older! Will I be talking like this to *my* children one day?

BRITISH RESERVE

Sir Eric helped himself to bacon and eggs. Hester poured out his coffee, and they sat down at the breakfast table[4]. Sir Eric unfolded *The Times*. Hester opened her letters. Once Hester asked her husband if he wanted any more coffee. Otherwise they did not talk.

At 8.30 Sir Eric looked at his watch.

'Well, I must be off, dear.'

He kissed Hester on the cheek and his man-servant[2] drove him to the station. The platform was full of middle-aged men wearing dark suits and carrying umbrellas. Like Sir Eric, they all had neatly folded newspapers under their arms, either *The Times* or *The Telegraph*. A few were wearing bowler hats.

They hardly greeted each other, though most of them knew one another, at least by sight. They did not shake hands[3].

The train came in, and they all got into first-class compartments. As soon as Sir Eric sat down, he unfolded his *Times*. So did the five other men who were with him. The two walls of newspaper which stretched across the compartment were not lowered until the train approached Waterloo an hour later. Not a word was spoken.

The return journey at 5.15 was no different, except that Sir Eric and his dark-suited companions were now reading evening newspapers.

CLOTHES AND FASHION

'Which is the boy and which is the girl?' Charles said, walking behind two long-haired young people who were both dressed in jeans and sweaters. 'I'm surprised so many girls don't trouble to dress up when they go out with their boyfriends.'

'It's one way they have of showing they're as tough and independent as men,' said Anne.

Charles was being unfair to the girls. Most British girls today take a great deal of interest in clothes and enjoy looking attractive. They are, in fact, far more fashion-conscious than their mothers were twenty years ago. Not so long ago English women had the reputation of being amongst the worst dressed women in Europe.

English men have always had the reputation for being smartly dressed, but modern boys are imitating their eighteenth-century ancestors[9] and now wear gaily patterned shirts and brightly coloured jackets and trousers. During the 1960s fashion shops for young people—called boutiques—were opened all over Britain, and London became the world's most important fashion centre for the young. More than half of the ten million foreign tourists who come to Britain every year are

Disapproval or incomprehension?

under thirty, and most of them never go further than London. Not only the girls go shopping. The boys go to Kensington, and also to King's Road, Chelsea. Many foreigners still go to Carnaby Street where the first men's boutiques were opened.

It is possible today to dress well without spending a great deal of money. Many boutiques and some big stores like Marks and Spencer's sell clothes which are both cheap and modern. You would find it difficult to guess from their clothes the social background of Christine, Penny or Susan—or Gareth and Jeremy.

MARRIAGE

Christine and Gareth sometimes talk about getting married soon.

'If we got married while you were at university,' said Christine, 'we'd manage quite well—with your grant and what I earned. You'd have to learn to cook, that's all, and do a bit of housework. And, of course, we wouldn't start a family until you got your degree.'

'If I were the housewife,' said Gareth, 'and you were bringing in the money, Mum'd think it highly unnatural! She'd be very shocked!'

'Well, you wouldn't let that stop you, would you?' said Christine.

A PARTY AT CHRISTINE'S HOUSE

'Mum and Dad have promised to go out and leave the house to us,' Christine told Gareth. 'Mum has left us plenty of cheese, sausages and fruit.'

The guests arrived in pairs. They each brought a bottle of beer or cider. There were ten people altogether. Gareth put on the record-player and they pushed back the chairs and tables in the living-room, so that those that wanted to could dance. A few pairs did dance, but most sat in corners and talked, with their arms round one another. Gareth and Christine stayed together, allowing the others to help themselves to the food and drink.

At one o'clock in the morning, Christine said, 'Let's go to the sea. Paul could drive us to Southend (see map p. 214) in his car.'

Paul, a mechanic from a local garage, was the owner of a 1938 Daimler.

'That old banger!¹⁰ It won't hold ten people!' Gareth said.

'Yes, it will,' said Christine. 'If it breaks down we'll push it!'

They all climbed into the Daimler and drove to Southend. It was mid-June and very hot.

'I feel like a bathe,' said Christine. Then she took Gareth's hand and they ran together into the sea with all their clothes on. The others followed, laughing and shouting.

THE TOWNSENDS HAVE A PARTY

'What time are they coming?' asked Leonard.

'About six o'clock,' replied Elizabeth. 'I put "from six to eight" on the invitation. Have you got the drinks ready? What are you offering them?'[5]

'The usual—sherry, gin and tonic or gin and Vermouth, and a special cocktail I've mixed.'

'You'd better move some of the chairs out of the sitting-room. It's going to be pretty crowded.'

The first guests arrived at 6.15. It's 'not done' to arrive at an English cocktail party punctually. By seven o'clock the Townsends' sitting-room, hall and stairs were packed with people. Nobody attempted to sit down. Glass in one hand, and cheese biscuit or sausage in the other, guests pushed their way through the crowd.

'Hello! Haven't seen you for ages. How's the family?'

'Fine! You look pretty fit. You've put on weight!'

Elizabeth and Leonard were too busy handing out drinks to do much introducing. The guests made their own introductions.

'I don't think we know each other. I'm Walter Mitford.'

'Didn't I see you at the Wilsons' last week?'

And so on.

'A nice party, don't you think?' said Leonard when the last guest had gone.

'Yes,' replied Elizabeth. 'I had an interesting talk with Robert Elleray about his new book.'

'Good heavens! Was Robert here? I never saw him!'

EVERYTHING STOPS FOR TEA[6]

One day, when Gwyn Williams reached the factory, he found that the women workers were threatening to leave.

'What's the matter, Doris?' he asked one of them.

'Maisy was "warned" by one of the foremen because she stayed too

66

long in the toilet yesterday,' Doris explained. 'He said she was doing her hair. How did he know? If they're going to stop us going to the toilet, we're going on strike.'

The men argued about whether they should join the women. They argued about it during the tea break in the morning, and during the tea break in the afternoon.

'It'd be more sensible to strike about our tea breaks,' said Gwyn. 'We don't get as long as the factory next door.'

'You're a lazy lot,' said the foreman. 'That's all you think about, your tea breaks!'

'Well, you can't expect a man to do a good day's work without his tea breaks!'

THE PATIENT BRITISH—QUEUING FOR BUSES

Mary Williams and her neighbour, Mrs Black, reached the bus stop after an afternoon's shopping in the West End. There were twenty people in front of them.

'We need an 88,' said Mary.

An 88 arrived at once. Everyone moved forward quickly.

'Two only!' said the conductor.

'Only eighteen people in front of us now!' Mary said to Mrs Black.

The next three 88s went straight by because they were full up.

'There are eighteen people *behind* us now!' said Mrs Black.

They waited ten minutes before another 88 arrived.

'Hurry along!' said the conductor. 'Two inside and plenty of room on top.'[11]

Mary and Mrs Black went upstairs.

'Two to Charing Cross, please,' Mary said to the conductor.

'Charing Cross?' he said. 'You'll have to get off at the next stop, dear. You're going in the wrong direction.'

PUBS[7]

Gwyn entered the Rose and Crown and went up to the bar.

'A pint of bitter, Jack,' he said.

The landlord filled a pint glass and pushed it across the counter. Gwyn drank his pint without taking breath and handed it to Jessie, the barmaid.

'Same again, Jessie,' he said.

'Thought you weren't coming tonight, Taff,' said Jessie. 'Been working late?'

Jessie, a good-looking, cheerful girl, is popular with the 'regulars' who come most nights to the Rose and Crown. The Rose and Crown is a working man's pub. It has not changed much since it was built at the end of the nineteenth century. It has the same dark brown walls and the same dark brown furniture. The seats are made of solid oak, and the few tables are stained with beer and cigarette burns. The men rarely sit down. They stand for most of the time, crowded round the bar.

After finishing his drink Gwyn went over to the dart board[8] where the Rose and Crown team were practising.

'Hurry up, Taff!' said one of them. 'Have you forgotten tomorrow's match?'

They played and drank beer for an hour and a half. The clock above the bar said 10.30 exactly.

'Time, gentlemen, please!' said the landlord.

There were cries of 'Come on, Jack! Just one more pint'. But the landlord was firm.

'It's closing time,' he said. 'I don't want any trouble with the law.'

'The coppers haven't been round for weeks, Jack!' Gwyn protested.

'All right!' said the landlord. 'Just a quick one—but someone had

A game of darts.

better have a look down the street. I've been caught once. I don't want to lose my licence.'

The Macdonalds, the Townsends, the Perkins, the young Blakeneys, the old Blakeneys, Gareth and Christine all go to pubs. Going to pubs is as much an English custom as going to cafés is a continental custom. There are city pubs for rich businessmen, where the seats are soft, and there are pink lights and bowls of flowers. There are simple 'out of the way' pubs where young people and artists go, and where you see nearly as many women as men. There are old country pubs (some date back to the fifteenth century) with solid beams and open wood fires, and there are plenty of plain, uncomfortable pubs—like Gwyn's Rose and Crown. Many pubs now offer food as well as drinks and some fashionable pubs serve expensive dinners.

NOTES
(1) *The Permissive Society*
A permissive society is one which allows a considerable amount of freedom, especially in matters concerning morality. In Britain today discipline at home and school has largely given way to 'freedom of expression' (i.e. self-expression) and young people of both sexes associate freely in a way not possible twenty years ago.

69

The British are well known for their love of animals. Here are two extremes of their attitude—on the one hand the numerous shows and competitions, on the other the fox hunt.

(2) *Servants*

Few British girls go into service. They prefer jobs in industry and the trades, because the wages are higher and there is more freedom. So the very few people who can afford living-in servants often employ foreigners who have come to Britain in search of jobs.

Many middle-income group families employ 'dailies', women who come in during the week to do the cleaning. Many of these families also have foreign 'au pair' girls. Officially an au pair girl is supposed to live as one of the family, receiving her keep, entertainment and pocket money—usually around £7 a week. In return she should help with the housework and care of any children. Hours and money are usually decided between the au pair girl and her employer. Au pair girls are actually supposed to put in about five hours a day, including baby-sitting, and must have one day off a week as well as time to attend English classes—which is, after all, their main reason for being here.

(3) *Hand-shaking and embracing*

English people rarely shake hands except when being introduced to someone for

the first time. They hardly ever shake hands with their friends—except when
seeing them after a long interval or saying goodbye before a long journey.
Whether to shake hands or not in England is sometimes a problem, even for
English people.

Englishmen rarely embrace one another—except after scoring goals in
football matches. Fathers do not even embrace their sons, except when they are
very little. This is one tradition that the young have not yet broken.

(4) *British meals mean different things and different times to different people*

Early morning	Breakfast
Midday	Lunch (hotels, restaurants, middle-class homes)
(12.00–2.00 p.m.)	Dinner (working class)
Mid-afternoon	Afternoon tea (hotels, tea-shops, middle-class homes)
(4.00–5.00 p.m.)	
Evening	
(5.30–6.30 p.m.)	High tea—light, early meal (middle class)
(5.30–6.30 p.m.)	Tea—main evening meal (working class)
(7.00–8.30 p.m.)	Supper (middle class)
(8.00–9.00 p.m.)	Dinner (hotels, restaurants, middle-class homes)
(9.00–10.00 p.m.)	Supper—light snack (working class)

At midday, lunch and dinner are exactly the same, and generally consist of two
courses.

In the evening, dinner is a large meal of at least three courses.

Supper is like dinner, but less grand. High tea is a mixture of tea and
supper—for example, meat, cheese and fruit may be added to bread and butter,
cakes and tea.

(5) *Drinks*

If you are invited to a drinks party, the party will probably be before dinner,
6.00–8.00 p.m. If you are invited by yourself to someone's house for a drink, it
will probably be after dinner, about 8.30 p.m. On a Sunday, you would be
invited for about 12.00 midday, and you might be the only guest—or there
might be a small party in progress. You would probably be offered wine, sherry,
gin and/or vermouth, or whisky on all these occasions. If you are invited to have
a pint of beer you will almost certainly arrange to meet in a particular pub.

71

(6) *Tea*

Britons drink a quarter of all the tea grown in the world each year. They are the world's greatest tea drinkers. Many of them drink it on at least eight different occasions during the day. They drink it between meals and at meals. They drink early-morning tea in bed—some early-morning tea drinkers have automatic tea-making machines connected to their alarm clocks.

(7) *Pub (short for Public House)*

The main drink served in pubs is beer, light or dark. Light beer is usually called bitter. Most pubs, of course, sell all kinds of alcohol, from whisky to wine. Many of them also offer light meals.

Most pubs have two drinking rooms, called bars—the public and the saloon bar, which is more comfortable and slightly more expensive. 'Bar' also means the counter at which the drinks are served.

Beer—and cider, a drink made from apples—is always sold in pint or half-pint glasses. A pint is equivalent to 0·57 litre.

No alcoholic drinks may be served to young people under eighteen, and no children under sixteen are allowed inside the bar.

Drinking Laws in Britain: There are hours during the day when alcoholic drinks cannot be served, either in pubs, hotels, restaurants or clubs. The usual opening hours for pubs (which may vary in different parts of the country) are:

England:	Cities:	11.00 a.m.–3.00 p.m.
		5.30 p.m.–11.00 p.m.
	Provinces:	11.00 a.m.–3.00 p.m.
		5.30 p.m.–10.30 p.m.
	Sundays, Christmas Day, Boxing Day.	$5\frac{1}{2}$ hours between earliest and latest permitted hours, with break between 3 and 5 p.m. After 5 p.m., not to exceed $3\frac{1}{2}$ hours, so … 7 – 10.30 p.m.
Wales:		Similar, but vary especially on Sundays. On Sundays no alcohol at all may be sold in some counties. As in Scotland, it is possible to go to a private hotel bar—even on a Sunday!
Scotland:	Weekdays:	11.00 a.m.–2.30 p.m.
		5.00 p.m.–10.00 p.m.
	Sundays:	Pubs not open at all.
		Hotels 12.30 p.m.–2.30 p.m.
		6.30 p.m.–10.00 p.m.

(8) *Darts*

A game in which small feathered arrows, called darts, are thrown at a board with numbered divisions on it. Most pubs have a dart board and any customer may play. Many pubs have a darts team which plays matches against teams from other pubs.

(9) *Fashion*

Though women's fashions change more often than men's, the following letter to *The Times* (2 March 1971) is a reminder that the present-day criticisms of young fashion is nothing new.

> 'Sir: When Lord Melbourne's second son William was a young teenager in 1794 he, like Henry Fox's son, was a worry to his father.
>
> Lord David Cecil tells us in *The Young Melbourne*, "He rebuked William when he first grew up for following the new-fangled fashion of short hair". *Plus ça change . . . !* '

In the late 1960s gangs of boys in the poorer districts of big industrial cities began to cut their hair really short. They called themselves 'skinheads' and declared war on the long-haired boys. Gang rivalry has been part of British city life since the early 1950s. Before the 'Skinheads', the 'Teddy Boys' imitated the style of dress of the Edwardian period (Edward VII, 1901–1910; the name Ted is short for Edward). The 'Mods and Rockers' were rival gangs whose rivalry took the form of riding either scooters or motorbikes. Now, gangs of young football fans wearing scarves with the colours of the club they support, fight rival fans, and often destroy property—even when they follow their clubs abroad.

(10) *'Banger'*

This is slang for an old second-hand car. This type of car is popular with young people. They often paint them in bright colours and give them names as a mark of affection, such as Geronimo, Flossy, or Fido. Old cars are not so easy to keep as they used to be, since every car three years old or more must receive a Ministry of Transport licence (M.O.T. for short)—in other words, it must be inspected every year and declared safe for use on the road.

(11) *Double-decker buses*

Most buses in British towns and cities are 'double-deckers'; this means they have an upstairs (on top) and a downstairs (inside). During the busiest times of the day a limited number of people are allowed to stand inside, but no one may

stand on top. Smoking is allowed on top, but not inside. The use of the word 'inside' for the lower deck (or floor) dates from the early days when the top deck was open, so that only passengers on the lower deck were inside.

QUESTIONS

(1) The young are now an important market for consumer goods. Has this, in your opinion, been a benefit to them?

(2) The British are often said to be cold and reserved. Do you believe in national characteristics of this kind? Can you give other examples?

(3) Do you agree with Jeremy that advertisements are often immoral? In what ways? Is it possible to defend the business of advertising?

(4) Are you as pessimistic as Susan about the future of the world?

(5) Many couples share the housework, and the money they earn, equally between them, as Gareth and Christine are planning to do. Do you think this is a good idea? Do you think it will become more normal?

FURTHER READING

Mabey, R.	The Pop Process (Hutchinson)
Newmark, P.	Out of your mind? *(Connexions)*
Gillott, J.	For better, for worse *(Connexions)*
	Behind the Scene *(Connexions)*
	The Penguin Private Eye
Bateman, M.	This England
McInnes, C.	Absolute Beginners (MacGibbon and Kee) (F)

4

Democracy and

Government

THE BRITISH CONSTITUTION

There is no written constitution. A thousand years ago, before the Norman Conquest in 1066, the Anglo-Saxon kings consulted the Great Council (an assembly of the leading men from each district) before taking major decisions. Between 1066 and 1215 the king ruled alone, but in 1215 the nobles forced King John to accept Magna Carta (the Great Charter), which took away some of the King's powers. In later centuries this was seen as the first occasion on which the king was *forced* to take advice. In 1264 the first parliament of nobles met together. Since then the British Constitution has evolved, in other words, it has grown up slowly, as a result of countless Acts of Parliament. There have been no violent changes in the constitution since the 'bloodless revolution' of 1688. Then, Parliament invited William and Mary to become Britain's first constitutional monarchs. A constitutional monarch is one who can rule only with the support of Parliament. The Bill of Rights (1689) was the first legal step towards constitutional monarchy. This Bill prevented the monarch from making laws or raising an army without Parliament's approval. Since 1689 the power of Parliament has grown steadily, while the power of the monarch has weakened. The Reform Acts of 1832, 1867 and 1884 gave the vote to large numbers of *male* citizens. Today every man and *woman* aged eighteen and over has the right to vote.

THE GOVERNMENT

The party that wins the most seats in a general election forms the government, and the leader of this party becomes *Prime Minister*, the

Magna Carta is now in the British Museum.

The Queen opening a new session of Parliament.

head of the government. The prime minister usually takes policy decisions with the agreement of his Cabinet (a committee of leading Ministers[1]). In recent years, partly influenced by the American presidential style, strong prime ministers have shown a tendency to take policy decisions on their own, but to do this successfully, the prime minister must later persuade either the Cabinet or a majority of his party to support his decision. He holds frequent Cabinet meetings at his house at number 10 Downing Street, which is very near the Houses of Parliament in Westminster. The power of the Cabinet is, in turn, controlled by Parliament, for no bill which a minister prepares can become law until it is passed by an Act of Parliament.

Bills can be introduced into either House (Notes 2 & 3). But all important bills are presented first to the House of Commons. Here they are explained and debated. If they receive a majority vote they go to the House of Lords. The House of Lords in turn debates and criticises them. It sometimes suggests changes, but it rarely votes against the government. For the Lords only have the power to delay the passing of a bill. They can throw out a bill once, but if it is presented to them a second time they must pass it.

Finally the bills are taken by the prime minister to the Queen, who always signs them. The Queen is a constitutional monarch, that is to say she governs through Parliament. She acts on the advice of her prime minister and does not make any major political decisions.

The House of Commons is the main law-making body. If a major bill is defeated there the government usually resigns and there is a new election. In any case, elections must be held at least every five years.

ELECTION DAY

All day long the official Labour and Conservative cars toured the constituency. Once during the afternoon the Labour car drove slowly down Royal Row, and a voice from a loud-speaker repeated, 'Vote for Moller. Vote Labour. Vote for the party that cares!' The Conservative car also drove down Royal Row, but Mary shut the window.

'We don't want to hear what *you* have to say!' she said.

At 6.30 Gwyn returned from work. He had come home by way of the polling station. Mary was sitting in front of the television with her feet up, drinking a cup of tea. Gareth was reading a book.

'Have you voted, Mary?' Gwyn asked.

'No,' said Mary, not taking her eyes off the screen. 'I've had a busy day. Anyway, my vote won't make any difference. Tom Moller is sure to get in.'

'You lazy so-and-so!' Gwyn said. 'You'd only vote if the polling station was right here in this house!'

'It's the television,' said Gareth. 'She's been watching it the whole afternoon!'

Gwyn turned to Gareth.

'Well, did you and your girlfriend enjoy voting for the first time?'

'We didn't vote,' replied Gareth. 'What's the point? Each party is as bad as the other.'

'Have you voted, Susan?' Sir Eric asked, when he returned from London.

'Well, I wasn't going to,' Susan said, 'but I did vote, actually!'

'Oh?' said Sir Eric.

'Yes. A woman in a car stopped me while I was going for a walk. I could tell she was a Conservative. She asked me if I'd like a lift to the polling station. The car was already almost full. She had the old Miss Moffits with her, and a man with a wooden leg. "Of course, our man is sure to get in!" she said, "but we must all vote, mustn't we?" "Yes," I said. "Thank you very much." But when I went in to the polling station I voted Labour—I mean, I had to, didn't I? It annoyed me. She was so sure I was a Conservative!'

Leonard Townsend recently interviewed Professor Stanbridge on British government for the British Overseas Broadcasting System. This is part of that programme.

LEONARD TOWNSEND: I have with me in the studio Professor Stanbridge, the distinguished American author of *Britain, Mother of Parliaments*. Professor Stanbridge, what interests you most about the British Constitution?

PROF STANBRIDGE: Its flexibility. Being an unwritten constitution, it can be 'bent' to suit any particular need. It has been said that the British Parliament can do anything except make a man a woman or a woman a man!

L.T: Can it be 'bent' to make a dictator, then?

PROF S: In theory, yes. In time of war, for example, Parliament allows the prime minister special authority. But in peace time no Parliament would dream of voting away its own power, and neither the monarch nor the prime minister could force it to do so.

L.T: But you claim in your book that Parliament does not have as much power as it ought to have.

PROF S: I don't think I said that. Parliament makes the laws of the country and therefore has great power, but the individual members of parliament have less power than they used to. There used to be more independent members and 'the Party' was not so strong. Now, when an important bill is presented to Parliament, M.P.s must vote in line with party orders. They *can* vote according to their conscience, or they can refuse to vote altogether. But if they rebel too often, they run the risk of being kicked out of their party. Also, if too many rebelled, or if the government had only a small majority in Parliament, they might cause their own party to lose office. I think that too much obedience to the party line gives too much power to the Cabinet and to the prime minister. Didn't a recent prime minister say 'Dogs have a licence to bark, but if they *bite* I take their licence away'?

L.T: But the 'dog who loses his licence' doesn't lose his seat in Parliament, does he?

PROF S: No, he doesn't, but he knows that at the next general election his party will not put him forward as a candidate. He could stand as an Independent, but in most cases his chances of winning on his own against the official party candidate would be small. His parliamentary career could be ruined.

L.T: Yes, but many backbenchers[4] do take this risk, and wouldn't you agree that in this way they have a considerable influence on ministers?

PROF S: Yes, I do agree. Members of the British Parliament have a strong sense of duty towards their country. It's an old and honoured tradition.

L.T: Well, people in Britain don't go into politics in order to make a fortune, do they!

PROF S: Hardly! An M.P.'s salary of £4,500* a year is nothing compared with the money he could make in business.

L.T: In your opinion, do M.P.s really speak for the people they represent?

PROF S: Well, many of them take a great interest in their constituencies.

*£5,750 in 1976.

They encourage people to come to them with complaints and suggestions, and visit their constituencies whenever they can.

L.T: So you think that the people in Britain really have a voice in politics?

PROF S: They have a voice all right, but they don't make the most of it. Very few people trouble to see their M.P.s and at election time large numbers of people don't vote at all, or vote for the wrong reasons. It was said—quite seriously—that when you lost the World Football Cup in 1970, many working people blamed the Labour government, and that was why a few days later Labour lost the election!

L.T: What is your opinion of our two-party system of government?

PROF S: Its chief disadvantage is that minority parties like the Liberals cannot be properly represented in Parliament. At the 1964 General Election the Liberals polled over three million votes, but had only nine members elected. (*See Note 7 for 1974 election results.*)

L.T: You are in favour of proportional representation[5] then?

PROF S: Not entirely. Proportional representation encourages the formation of new or 'break-away' parties, that is, groups of people who separate from the main parties and form their own party. This can lead to confusion. I think it is a good thing for one party to have a clear majority and not to have to depend on other parties for support. In other words, I don't think that coalition governments are satisfactory.

L.T: It has been said that in our modern world monarchies are out of date. Do you think we British should replace our monarch with an elected president?

PROF S: No. Your Queen is a symbol of the permanence of your constitution. Although she hasn't any power she prevents any other single person from having it—just by being there. Besides, she is above party politics, and is regarded with affection and admiration by people from all parties.

L.T: You are not shocked by the cost of the monarchy to the nation?

PROF S: Certainly not! Royalty earns much more for Britain than it costs. It's one of the great tourist attractions. Isn't the Changing of the Guard at Buckingham Palace one of the first things foreign tourists go and see? In any case, your Queen, and the other members of the Royal Family, earn their salaries by hard work. They're always entertaining foreign heads of state, opening new universities, and factories, going on goodwill tours of the Commonwealth and so on. Oh no! Becoming a republic wouldn't make you more democratic in any way.

CHARLES TAKES A FRIEND TO THE HOUSE OF COMMONS

Charles has many foreign friends who, from time to time, come to England on business. Last month Carlos Garcia came over from South America and Charles took him to hear a debate in the House of Commons.

When they sat down in the Public Gallery, a member was on his feet addressing the House. Carlos listened for a moment. Then he turned to Charles.

'But a lot of them aren't paying attention to him!' he said.

'They don't have to,' replied Charles. 'It's all being written down. They'll be able to read it in the official report tomorrow.'

A couple of ministers on the front benches had their feet up on the tables. So had one of the Opposition leaders who was facing them across the floor. Several M.P.s were reading or marking papers and two others were chatting and laughing together.

'What happens when they get too noisy?' asked Carlos.

'The Speaker deals with them,' said Charles. 'That's the man sitting in the middle of the House with the long wig on. He's elected by the House of Commons, and though he belongs to one of the parties, he has to give up all party loyalties. He never votes except when the votes are equal. Then he gives the deciding vote. It's his job to keep order. Members usually obey him!'

The member addressing the House went on talking.

'In view of the danger to health, it seems a small sacrifice to ask the public to give up smoking in places of entertainment,' he said. 'After all, we're not allowed to smoke here.'

A member looked up from his papers.

'Does the Honourable Member think of this House, then, as "a place of entertainment"?'

There was a roar of laughter. Charles explained to Carlos that the 'Honourable Member' was introducing a bill to make smoking illegal in theatres, cinemas and other public places.

A few days later Carlos read in *The Times* that the anti-smoking bill had been defeated by 300 votes to 120.

'But the man we heard introducing it belonged to the government party!' said Carlos. 'Members of his own party must have voted against him.'

Charles explained that it was a private member's bill, that is to say, a bill not introduced by a member of the Cabinet. Members from both sides of the House have the right to introduce private bills, although they often have to wait a long time before their turn comes round.

'M.P.s are free to vote as they like with private members' bills,' Charles explained. 'There are no party orders. It's an important part of our democracy. Some of our most useful laws have been passed in this way.'

THE CIVIL SERVICE

Civil servants are professional 'servants' of the state. They run the various government departments, advise the ministers and carry out their policies. Since they are non-political and permanent, they cannot be dismissed when ministers or governments change.

The most important ministries and departments of the civil service are in Whitehall, the broad street which leads down to the Houses of Parliament in Westminster. Just as the name 'Westminster' is often used to mean 'Parliament', so 'Whitehall' often means 'the government' or 'the civil service'. The British civil service has a reputation for honesty, but to most of the British people it also suggests bureaucracy— government by paid state officials rather than by persons elected by the people.

LOCAL GOVERNMENT

In 1974 the map of Britain was redrawn (see map page viii). The familiar pattern of counties is no longer the same. New counties have been created—Avon, Cumbria, the Western Isles (Scotland), but many of the old names are still there (see map). The purpose of this replanning was to make local government more efficient.

The County Council remains the most important unit of local government. It is in charge of the county as a whole. Nobody can plan anything, neither shopping-centres, nor factories, nor parks, nor race courses without the permission of the County Council. Its other responsibilities include roads (except motorways and A roads); transport (the bus services); the police; the fire service; education—it builds the schools, pays the teachers and decides what kind of educational system the county will have (see L.E.A.s, Chapter 9); personal social services including old people's homes, child welfare etc.

Each county is now divided into districts of between 60,000 and 100,000 people. The District Councils are responsible for housing, especially for the building and renting of council houses. It is their job to keep the district clean and to inspect the food shops. And it is they who employ the dustmen who go from house to house to collect rubbish.

The new District Councils are larger than the old councils they replaced, but on the whole they are not as bureaucratic as some people feared. If a person needs information about planning permission for a new house he can still call at the local council office. If he wants to get rid of a lot of old iron, the council will usually do it for him willingly — just as they will get rid of rats from his yard. The British have never liked faceless, unapproachable officials.

County and District Councils are run by part-time unpaid councillors, who are elected in the same way as M.P.s. Although most of them represent a political party, they don't often have political battles among themselves. But the government is not pleased if the opposition party gets control of the majority of local councils. The councillors appoint from among themselves the committees who run the different departments. They also appoint paid full-time officials. These officials, like the civil servants, are completely non-political. The head of each county council and district council is called the 'chairman'. The chairman is appointed every year by his councillors.

The money the councils need comes from the rates. Rates are paid by everybody who owns or rents a building or land. How much a person pays depends on the value of the property. The councils also get a large general grant from the Treasury (the finance department of the government). The government never refuses to give this grant because it disapproves of a council's politics, but it may hesitate if it feels the money is being spent unwisely. Some councils are more progressive than others, and, with a few scandalous exceptions, most councillors are honest and conscientious.

NOTES
(1) *The Cabinet*
Each new prime minister may make changes in the size of his cabinet and may

create new ministries or make other changes. The diagram below illustrates the Cabinet as organised by the Labour Prime Minister, Harold Wilson, in November 1975. There are also a number of Ministers who are not in the Cabinet (in 1975 there were twenty-nine).

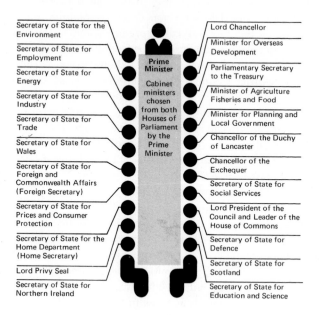

(2) *House of Lords*

Hereditary Peers :	Dukes (26 plus 4 Royal Dukes), Marquesses (37), Earls (176), Viscounts (116), Barons (468), Peeresses in their own right (19).
Life Peers (202), Life Peeresses (33).	
Archbishops (2), Senior Bishops (24).	

The figures given above are as they were in 1975. Life peers (Lords) and peeresses receive their peerages as a reward for service, and their children do not inherit the title. Peers may not sit in the House of Commons as M.P.s, but in 1963 the Peerage Act made it possible for peers to give up their peerages. For example, in 1963 the Conservative Party, which at that time formed the government, chose as its new leader the Earl of Home, who then became prime minister. It would have been difficult for a prime minister to sit in the House of Lords, and so the Earl gave up his title and was elected to the House of Commons as Sir Alec Douglas-Home.

(3) *House of Commons*

Government	Opposition
635 Elected Members of Parliament (M.P.s)	

The elected members represent 635 constituencies in England, Wales, Scotland and Northern Ireland. The size of the constituencies varies, the average being about 60,000 electors. Everyone of the age of eighteen or over has the right to vote and to belong to any political party. Although there is no limit to the number of political parties, in effect, Britain has a two-party system of government, since most people vote either Conservative or Labour. The last Liberal prime minister was the Welshman, Lloyd George, whose defeat in 1922 marked the end of Liberal power. Since that time very few Liberal M.P.s have been elected. In the October 1974 election the number of Liberal M.P.s was reduced from 14 to 13, although this number does not truly reflect the number of votes given to Liberal candidates (see Note 7).

In a British election the candidate who wins the most votes is elected, even if he or she does not get as many as the combined votes of the other candidates. One of the close results in the October 1974 election was in the Drake constituency at Plymouth, where the Conservative candidate was elected. The results were:

Miss J. E. Fookes (Conservative)	17,287
B. W. Fletcher (Labour)	17,253
Miss M. E. Castle (Liberal)	7,354

The Conservative candidate had a majority of 34 over her nearest rival and won a seat in Parliament, but 24,607 people voted for other candidates and so indirectly against her.

(4) *Backbenchers*: 'Bench' means 'seat', and the backbenchers in the House of Commons are the ordinary members of Parliament who sit on the seats behind the front benches. In the House, the government seats are on one side of the Speaker and the opposition seats are on the other side. The two front benches are occupied by government ministers and their opposite numbers on the other side (the 'Shadow Cabinet' of the opposition).

(5) *Proportional Representation*: This is an election system which seeks to give minority parties representation in Parliament. It aims to give each party a proportion of seats in Parliament corresponding to the proportion of votes it receives in an election. For example, a minority party receiving 5 per cent of the votes at a general election should get 5 per cent of the seats. A large party with 40 per cent of the votes should get 40 per cent of the seats. The system would be easy to work if everybody voted directly for a party, instead of voting for an individual candidate in a constituency. This would mean, however, that there was no true connection between the voters and their M.P.s. The large parties fear that under this system they could rule only in coalition—that is with the

85

help of a small party. Under the present system a party receiving a minority share of the votes can still get a big majority of the seats in Parliament[3]. Japan, Sweden, France and West Germany, among others, all have different systems of proportional representation.

(6) *Election results since 1951*

	1951	1955	1959	1964	1966	1970	Feb. 1974	Oct. 1974
Labour	*295*	277	258	*317*	*363*	287	*301*	*319*
Conservative	*321*	*345*	*365*	303	253	*330*	296	276
Liberal	6	6	6	9	13	6	14	13
Independent			1			5		1
Independent Labour							1	
Democratic Labour							1	
Irish Nationalist	2	2						
Irish Labour	1							
Republican Labour (Northern Ireland)					1			
Ulster Unionists							11	10
Social Democratic and Labour Party (Northern Ireland)							1	1
Scottish National Party						1	7	11
Plaid Cymru							2	3
Speaker	1	1	1	1	1	1	1	1

(Italics show the party which formed the government)

Note: in 1970 Conservative M.P.s included 7 Ulster Unionist, but not in 1974. After Sunningdale the 3 Loyalist parties formed the United Ulster Unionist Council and won 11 of the 12 Ulster seats.

(7) *Votes at 1970 and 1974 elections*

Party	1970	% of votes	February 1974	% of votes	October 1974	% of votes
Labour	12,179,166	42·8	11,634,726	37·2	11,458,704	39·3
Conservative	13,144,692	46·4	11,963,207	38·2	10,458,548	35·8
Liberal	2,117,638	7·5	6,063,470	19·3	5,348,193	18·3
Other	903,311	3·2	1,651,823	5·3	1,867,637	6·6

Note that although Labour polled fewer votes than the Conservatives in the February 1974 election, they gained more seats in the House of Commons and formed a minority government, after Edward Heath (leader of the Conservatives) had been unable to form a coalition with the Liberals. Minority governments or governments with very narrow majorities have not usually lasted very long in Britain. They may lose seats at bye-elections (when an M.P. retires or dies, there is always a new election in his constituency). In October 1974 the Labour prime minister, Harold Wilson, called an election to try to increase the number of Labour M.P.s. Although he was successful, he still did not have an overall majority in the House of Commons. However, he was able to form a minority government which carried out its programme because the other parties could not agree to oppose the government on any major matter and so outvote it in the Commons.

Note also the steady increase in the votes for 'other' parties. This has been due largely to a rise in the popularity of the Welsh and Scottish Nationalist parties.

(8) *Prime Ministers since 1951*

1951	1955	1957, 1959	1963
W. S. Churchill (C.)	A. Eden (C.)	H. Macmillan (C.)	Sir A. Douglas-Home (C.)
1964, 1966	1970	1974 (February, October)	April, 1976
H. Wilson (Lab.)	E. Heath (C.)	H. Wilson (Lab.)	J. Callaghan (Lab.) (took over on H. Wilson's retirement)

(9) The economic crisis in 1976 widened the division between the Labour Left-wing and the Labour Right-wing. The Right-wingers were regarded by most people outside the Party as moderate. The Left-wingers were considered by many as extremist. They protested vigorously against the cuts in public spending (education, housing, welfare, etc.) which were introduced by the Chancellor, Denis Healey. They were shocked by the rise in unemployment, which reached $1\frac{1}{2}$ million in August 1976. But the Prime Minister was determined to go ahead with his plan to 'save Britain', the cornerstone of which was the 'Social Contract' agreed between the government and the T.U.C. (see p. 109, Note 2). According to the Social Contract, the T.U.C. accepted that wages must be controlled and must not jump ahead of prices.

In 1975 the Conservatives voted for a new leader, Margaret Thatcher, the first woman party political leader in Britain who is more to the right than her predecessor, Edward Heath. In 1976 the Liberals, too, voted for a new leader, David Steel.

(10) *Local Government*

Some larger towns form one single district. Not counting London, there are also six metropolitan counties—huge built-up areas centred on the big cities. These are divided into districts called 'boroughs' (e.g. Stockport Borough) or, if they are big enough, they are called 'cities' (e.g. Manchester City). Metropolitan boroughs and cities have populations of over 250,000 and, because of their size, they are responsible for their own education, personal social services, libraries etc.

QUESTIONS
(1) The monarch has no power in British government. What, then, is she there for?
(2) The House of Lords has the power to delay a bill, but the Lords cannot prevent the passing of a law. What are the advantages of this system?
(3) Should people be allowed to vote at eighteen?
(4) How does the election system in your country compare with the British system?

FURTHER READING

Harvey and Bather	The British Constitution (Macmillan)
Mackenzie, K.	The English Parliament
Taylor, E.	The House of Commons at Work
Jackson, W. E.	Local Government in England and Wales
Princess Marie-Louise	My Memories of Six Reigns
Snow, C. P.	Corridors of Power (F)
Edelman, M.	The Minister (F)

5
Welfare and
Charity

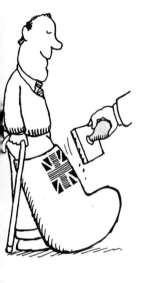

WELFARE

One day when Jeremy was taking some
foreign friends round London, one of them
was knocked down by a bus. He was taken to
hospital, where it was found that his injuries
were serious. He was operated on and kept
in hospital for more than a month. Specialists
visited him and he was given expensive drugs. When he finally left
hospital he received no bill at all, for Britain is a welfare state and
foreign visitors receive the same free medical attention as Britons do
themselves.

The British Welfare State was planned during the second world war
by the economist, William Beveridge. The Labour government of
1945–50 passed laws giving the country almost everything for which
Beveridge asked. The Conservative governments which followed also
accepted the Beveridge Plan and made no basic changes.

'Welfare' means 'health, comfort and freedom from want'. A welfare
state attempts to give all this to every member of the community, and it
pays the cost out of taxes of various kinds[1]. It is like an immense
insurance company with which every single citizen is compulsorily
insured.

The welfare service in Britain provides allowances and pensions[2], so
that no man need fear that his family will starve if he loses his job, or falls
sick, or has to retire. There are centres to which people can go for help
and advice about their marriages, their children, their careers.
Specially trained social workers help poor people who are in trouble.

When the Macdonald twins were babies, Peggy took them once a

The National Health Service provides for people of all ages—from children at family health clinics to old people in rest homes.

week to her local welfare centre, where a doctor examined them, weighed them and advised her about their feeding. She could also get baby food at reduced prices.

Some people criticise the welfare state for being too generous. Others claim that it is not generous enough.

'The British working man is getting too lazy,' said Herbert Perkins. 'He stops work if he's got a pain in his toe! What we need is a bit more healthy competition and a bit more healthy fear of unemployment.'

Elizabeth Townsend feels differently.

'It's true that some men can get more money from the welfare state than by working,' she said, 'but that's not because unemployment and family allowances are too generous. It's because our lowest paid workers get such miserable wages. Some of them earn only just enough to buy the bare necessities. Anyway our family allowances are less than in most Common Market countries. But there's still much too big a gap between the top and the bottom income groups in this country.'

Elizabeth also feels that more ought to be done for old people. She would like to see more decent homes and hostels for them. The care of lonely, neglected old people is one of the biggest problems of the British welfare state.

THE NATIONAL HEALTH SERVICE (N.H.S.)

The Macdonalds' doctor, Dr Miller, is one of five local doctors who have joined together to form a group practice. Many National Health Service doctors belong to group practices. They share the surgery where patients come to visit them, and they share duties in such a way that each doctor can have one complete day off a week.

Non-specialist doctors like Dr Miller are called general practitioners (G.P.s for short). Dr Miller, being a Health Service G.P., is paid by the state. He has about 2,500 patients on his list, but, fortunately for him, only a small proportion of them come to see him regularly.

However, Dr Miller sees a lot of the Macdonalds. Jane had a serious operation when she was five, and the doctor visited her frequently at home after she left hospital. For these visits and the hospital treatment the Macdonalds did not have to pay anything. Besides this, Ian is a diabetic and needs a continual supply of drugs. These drugs cost Ian nothing, because patients who need a life-saving drug of this kind are not charged. For all other drugs there is a small fixed charge. For example Ian's mother, who sleeps badly, gets her sleeping pills for hardly more than £2 a year, for doctors often write out a month's supply of medicine on one prescription[3].

The Macdonalds have other reasons, too, for being glad there is a National Health Service. Ian's mother has bad teeth and went to the dentist fifteen times last year. For this treatment she only paid £10. The twins have their teeth examined at school for nothing[4]. Ian, who is short-sighted, wears National Health glasses which cost him only £5.60, and Douglas is young enough to get his glasses for nothing.

However, Ian's mother complains about the Health Service nearly every time she goes to see the doctor.

'I spent an hour at the surgery this morning waiting to see Dr Miller, and when my turn came he gave me only three minutes. He said there was nothing the matter with me.'

'Well, there wasn't, was there, Mother?' said Ian.

'It was better in the old days, when we had our family doctor,' said Mrs Macdonald.

The simplest beauty treatment we know.
Fifteen minutes, twice a year

Regular check-ups
save your teeth...
and save your money.

'But you didn't go to see him so often then, did you, because you had to pay each time you saw him!'

'I think you're very ungrateful,' said Peggy. 'Do you realise that if we had been living in some countries, Jane's illness would have ruined us? It would have cost us hundreds of pounds. And you're not fair to Dr Miller. He works exceptionally hard, but he's not nearly as rich as he would be if he had a private practice in America or France.'

Nobody pretends that the National Health Service in Britain is perfect. Nurses have a hard job, and junior hospital doctors sometimes have to work 90 hours a week. They were so dissatisfied in the mid 1970s that both groups protested and demonstrated in order to get better pay and better conditions.

Many old-fashioned, overcrowded hospitals need to be improved.

'There still aren't enough beds,' Peggy said. 'I had to wait six months for an operation on my knee. Of course, if it had been urgent, they would have operated at once, but that's no excuse.'

Wealthy people, like the Blakeneys, go to private doctors, or see specialists in Harley Street, the famous doctors' street in London. When they are ill they go to private clinics, where they pay £150 a week or more.

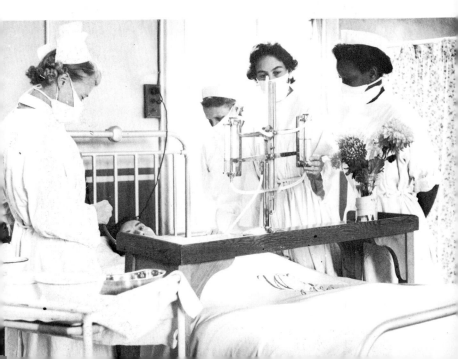

Nearly all the Harley Street specialists have posts in the big London hospitals, where they operate on, and look after Health Service patients free of charge. Most hospitals also have a few private (or 'pay') beds, so that the specialists can look after their private patients and their N.H.S. patients under the same roof. In 1975 the Labour Government announced that there must be an end to 'pay' beds in N.H.S. hospitals. The specialists threatened to leave the N.H.S. if the government interfered with their private practices.

'The specialists may lose the battle of the pay beds one day, but they'll never leave the Health Service!' Peggy said.

HOUSING

Housing (the bad condition of many houses as well as the lack of houses) is one of the biggest problems of the welfare state. The chief responsibility for housing the less well-off people lies with the district councils. But between 1971 and 1973 the local councils built only one third of all new houses. In some poor districts owners and tenants pay very low rates (see p. 82) because of the condition of their houses. Sadly, this means district councils which need the money most, have much less to spend than the councils which need it less. On top of this, government spending cuts, announced in 1976, mean grants to district councils will be severely reduced.

Nearly half the houses in Britain are owned by the people who live in them. About one third are owned by the local authorities, and the rest are rented from private owners. A typical rent for a two-bedroomed council house is £6 a week. The rent of an old property can be as low as £4. But in some new council estates it can be as high as £9 a week. Rents vary from council to council. A two-bedroomed house can be built for about £7,500 (twice that amount in a rich district). People who have a little capital can borrow 95 per cent of the cost of the house from building societies. But large mortgages may take 20 to 30 years to pay off.

Since the second world war a number of completely new towns have been built. Most of these new towns are on the edge of country villages or small market towns. They have been carefully planned, with traffic-free shopping centres. The houses are in tree-lined streets or grouped around open spaces. Each town is self-contained, with its own hospitals, churches, schools, colleges and industries. The factories are all grouped together in an 'industrial area'. The purpose of the new towns is to attract people and industry away from the crowded cities and to found whole new communities, but the new towns have only scratched at the surface of the housing problem. Besides, some people find them lonely and unfriendly places.

Housing was the subject of an interview which Leonard Townsend had with Mrs Partridge, a sociologist, and Mr Pollard, a councillor of one of the new towns.

LEONARD TOWNSEND: Mrs Partridge, I understand that you are very concerned about the housing situation in Britain.

MRS PARTRIDGE: Indeed I am. The government itself admits that there are more than two million houses which ought to be pulled down at once. It also admits that there are another two million in such a shocking state that it would be a waste of money to repair them.

L.T: What do you mean by 'shocking state'?

MRS P: I mean houses that are in such a bad condition that they are permanently damp, or houses where you'll find as many as five families sharing one tap and one toilet.

MR POLLARD: But what about all the good things that have been and are being done? What about the rebuilding of whole parts of cities like Sheffield and Birmingham and Coventry—not to mention the new towns?

MRS P: That's all very fine and splendid, but it's only one side of the picture. I'm simply saying that we're not doing enough. We can feel proud of what is good, but surely we shouldn't be proud that, for example, Glasgow is sometimes called the biggest slum in Western Europe?

L.T: What you are saying, in effect, Mrs Partridge, is that the housing in this country isn't worthy of a welfare state!

MRS P: Exactly! According to government figures there are less than 20,000 homeless people, but thousands more are living in such terrible conditions that they ought to be classed as homeless. It isn't that these people can't afford a reasonable rent. There just aren't enough houses.

L.T: Whom do you blame?

MRS P: The government, for not providing enough money, and the councils for not spending properly what there is.

MR P: Aren't you being unfair to the local housing committees? Many of

95

them do wonderful work.

MRS P: I agree, but that doesn't excuse councils that are inefficient and don't take enough interest. Don't you think it is shocking that in modern Britain there are still families who have nowhere to live? Do you think it's right that whole families should have to sleep in the ruins of empty buildings or under bridges or in railway station waiting-rooms?

MR P: But there are excellent hostels where they can go.

MRS P: In some towns, perhaps, Mr Pollard, but things are very different in many of our midland and northern industrial cities, and in parts of London. Even where there *are* places, some of the state-run homes for the homeless are less comfortable than prisons. In any case, my point is that we shouldn't need so many hostels for homeless families because there shouldn't be any homeless families!

L.T: Mrs Partridge, I think many people would say that you are exaggerating and drawing attention to the worst housing conditions instead of looking at the situation as a whole. Would you agree that you belong to a 'pressure group' which is trying to bring pressure on the government to do something about the housing problem?

MRS P: If that's what belonging to a pressure group means, the answer is 'yes'! But I'm *not* exaggerating. Housing is the most serious problem of our welfare state. If it weren't, would we hear so much about that excellent charity, Shelter, which does such wonderful work in finding homes for the homeless?

CHARITIES

Britain's welfare services still cannot protect people against want as completely as Beveridge had hoped. That is why there are so many charities—private organisations founded to support an immense variety of causes which get no support (or not enough) from the state.

There are over 60,000 charities. Some are run by a handful of people and collect only a few hundred pounds a year. The big ones have an army of helpers and collect millions of pounds[5].

Hester Blakeney organises the local branch of the Save the Children Fund[6]. She and her helpers collect clothes for children. They raise money in all kinds of different ways. Once a year they organise a big sale in the local town hall. They invite all their friends to morning coffee

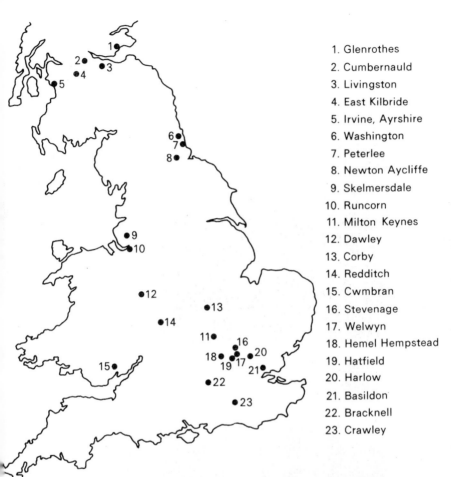

1. Glenrothes
2. Cumbernauld
3. Livingston
4. East Kilbride
5. Irvine, Ayrshire
6. Washington
7. Peterlee
8. Newton Aycliffe
9. Skelmersdale
10. Runcorn
11. Milton Keynes
12. Dawley
13. Corby
14. Redditch
15. Cwmbran
16. Stevenage
17. Welwyn
18. Hemel Hempstead
19. Hatfield
20. Harlow
21. Basildon
22. Bracknell
23. Crawley

The map shows where the new towns are. The architecture of Cumbernauld.

parties—and ask them to pay. Last year they managed to raise £3,700 and fill sixty sacks with clothing.

This kid
can't wait to get to school
...because home is nothing but hell

Help SHELTER get her out of the slums and into a decent home
9-16 OCTOBER IS SHELTER WEEK

SHELTER National Campaign for the Homeless

NOTES
(1) *How money for welfare is raised*
Every working man and woman of sixteen and over, and earning £13 or more, pays 5.75% of his/her weekly earnings up to £95 a week. This is taken off the weekly pay packet. His/her employer pays 8.75%. Married women can pay full contributions, or 2% of their earnings. (If they pay 2%, they rely on their

husbands' contribution for maternity grant, retirement pension and death grant.) There is a different form of payment for self-employed people. The rest of the money comes from rates and taxes.

(2) *Benefits and Pensions*
    a) Unemployment benefit
    b) Sickness benefit
    c) Maternity benefits—a woman who is going to have a child is given a maternity grant and an allowance.
    d) Widow's benefits—if a woman is under sixty when her husband dies she receives an allowance for herself and for any children still dependent on her. When the allowance ends, she will receive a pension if she was over forty at the time of her husband's death.
    e) Child benefit
    f) Supplementary benefit—for people in difficulties on low income.
    g) Retirement pension   h) Death grant
Self-employed people do not qualify for unemployment benefit.

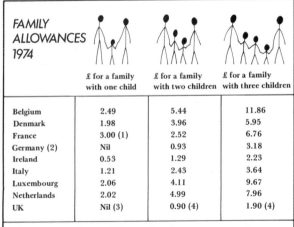

FAMILY ALLOWANCES 1974	£ for a family with one child	£ for a family with two children	£ for a family with three children
Belgium	2.49	5.44	11.86
Denmark	1.98	3.96	5.95
France	3.00 (1)	2.52	6.76
Germany (2)	Nil	0.93	3.18
Ireland	0.53	1.29	2.23
Italy	1.21	2.43	3.64
Luxembourg	2.06	4.11	9.67
Netherlands	2.02	4.99	7.96
UK	Nil (3)	0.90 (4)	1.90 (4)

(1) The allowance for one child is payable only to one-parent families.
(2) Only payable if weekly income is below £57
(3) Allowance for one child to be introduced in 1977.
(4) Increased to £1.50 and £3.00 respectively in 1976.

(3) *Prescription*
This is the written order for medicine which a doctor gives to a patient. A patient who is given a prescription by a G.P. usually goes to a chemist's for the medicine. Originally, medicine was supplied free under the National Health

Service. Small charges were introduced as costs rose, both Conservative and Labour governments adding to the increases. In 1971 the charge was increased from 12½p to 20p per item on the prescription.

(4) Dental Service

Like doctors, dentists may take part in the National Health Service and may also have private patients. There are an increasing number of group practices. A patient may pay anything up to £3.50 for a course of treatment, and up to a maximum of £12 for false teeth.

(5) Charities (some of the best known)

Dr Barnado's—helps children in need, owns homes, arranges adoptions.
CARE—looks after mentally handicapped.
Oxfam—relieves suffering all over the world, especially in times of disaster.
Child Poverty Action Group—CPAG
Church of England Children's Society—provides homes for orphans (children without parents) and gives help of all kinds. Runs homes, special schools, hostels. Largest adoption society in Britain.
Shelter—searches for homes for the homeless.
St Dunstan's—helps men and women blinded on war service.
NSPCC (The National Society for the Prevention of Cruelty to Children)
RSPCA (The Royal Society for the Prevention of Cruelty to Animals)
RSPB (The Royal Society for the Protection of Birds)
Spastics Society
Cancer Research Fund

(6) Save the Children Fund

—international, non-political, non-religious organisation founded by an English woman in 1919. Its aims are (a) to help save children's lives wherever they are threatened by bad conditions or great suffering, (b) to raise the standard of child care and protection all over the world.

(7) Some examples of Public Expenditure 1973–74 (£ millions)

Health and Personal Services	£3,612
Social Security	£5,533
Education, Libraries, Science and Arts	£4,529
Defence	£3,456

(8) Food and Health

The World Health Organisation claims that the food a person eats each day must contain at least 1,500 calories to keep him in good health. In Britain the average for each person is 3,150 calories.

(9) Expectation of Life (a selection of the highest and lowest figures from each continent)

	Country	Year	Male	Female
Africa	Chad	1963–4	29	35
	Gabon	1960–1	25	45
	UAR	1960	51·6	53·8
	Kenya	1969	46·9	51·2
N. America	USA	1972	67·4	75·2
	Canada	1965–67	68·75	75·18
S. America	Argentine	1965–70	64·06	70·22
	Equador	1961–63	51	53·6
	Peru	1960–65	52·59	55·48
	Venezuela	1961	66·41	66·41
Asia	Sri Lanka	1967	64·8	66·9
	India	1951–60	41·89	40·55
	Indonesia	1960	47·5	47·5
	Japan	1972	70·49	75·92
	Jordan	1959–63	52·6	52
Europe	E. Germany	1969–70	68·85	74·19
	W. Germany	1968–70	67·24	73·44
	Sweden	1972	71·97	77·41
	UK	1970–72	68·9	75·1
	Yugoslavia	1970–71	65·30	70·14

The Netherlands, Denmark, Norway, Iceland all have a male expectation of life over 70·5 years. Sweden has the highest expectation of life (both male and female) in the world.

	Country	Year	Male	Female
Oceania	Australia	1960–62	67·92	74·18
—	USSR	1968–9	65	74

QUESTIONS
(1) Does a welfare state make people lazy, or too dependent on government help?
(2) How does the N.H.S. compare with the medical services in your country?
(3) Does society have a duty to provide houses for the homeless?
(4) If you had a limited amount of time and money, which of the charities on p. 100 would you support?

FURTHER READING

Fairbrother	Shelter *(Connexions)*
Coates and Silburn	Poverty: The Forgotten Englishmen
Martin, I.	From Workhouse to Welfare *(Topics in History)*
Ferris, P.	The Doctors
Orwell, G.	Keep the Aspidistra Flying (F)
Greenwood, W. O.	Love on the Dole (F)

Two aspects of the world of big business—a mass meeting of car workers during a strike, and the new London Stock Exchange.

6

Business, Trade and Trade Unions

GWYN AND HIS MATES AT THE PINNER FACTORY
When Gwyn arrived at the factory one morning, he saw a crowd in front of the notice-board.

'What's up?' said Gwyn.

'A merger!' replied one of his mates. 'Pinner's are joining up with Northern Electrics!'

'Northern Electrics? They've already merged with Blacketts and Pollards. Who else are they going to eat up? They're bigger than Pinners. Anyway, last year's figures were the worst ever. They could close this factory down.'

'Why this factory?'

'Because we're the least efficient factory in the Pinner group,' said the foreman. 'They'll want to put all their money into the new north London factory.'

'So we'll lose our jobs and become redundant!' said Gwyn.

'There'll be jobs for some of you in the north London factory,' said the foreman. 'As for the rest of you, you'll get other jobs all right—and you'll get redundancy pay. You'll be better off.'

'Other jobs?' said Gwyn's mate. 'We'll be lucky if we find any jobs at all. What about my hire-purchase payments? I've just bought a new car, and a new cooker for the wife. That means I'm paying £14 a week and I'll have to go on paying it for the next two years!'

'Yes, and I'm still paying for our new chairs,' said Gwyn.

'You won't have to worry, Gwyn,' said the foreman. 'They'll need panel-beaters at the other factory.'

'But I don't want to have to go and live in north London!'

There were cries of agreement. Nobody wanted to move.

'You are a conservative lot!' said the foreman. 'Don't want a different job! Don't want to move!'

'It's all right for you,' said a woman. 'With the money you earn you'll be able to buy a house. People like us'll have to live in council houses, but in the other place we'll be at the bottom of the housing list. We'll have to wait months for a proper home.'

'Yes,' said another woman, 'and what about all our friends?'

'And what about the pub?' said Gwyn.

'They have pubs in north London!' said the foreman.

'Yes, but have they got a darts team like the one at the Rose and Crown?'

At that moment the shop steward arrived. A shop steward represents the factory workers in any discussions with management.

'I say we oughtn't to support the merger unless the management promises there'll be no redundancies,' he said. 'They want a merger because it'll make bigger profits for the shareholders.'

'If they make bigger profits,' said the foreman, 'they'll be able to spend more money on making the factories more efficient. Then they'll sell more washing machines and we'll get higher wages.'

'They'll only sell more if we work harder,' said an older worker. 'The average worker in the other Common Market countries produces much more a year than the average British worker, and better stuff, too. We're lazy!'

'That's because they have better conditions, better houses and better pay,' the shop steward said, 'and a minimum wage.'

'Quite right,' one of the women said. 'The Dutch and the Germans are much better off than us—better pensions, better sick pay, longer holidays with pay, more modern factories—the lot.'

'Well, if a merger means closing this factory,' said the shop steward, 'I'll call a meeting and I'll get 'em all to come out on strike, you'll see.'

If the workers in Gwyn's factory agreed to go on strike against the advice of their unions it would be an unofficial 'wildcat' strike, and they would get no strike pay from their unions. But their families would get enough to live on from supplementary benefits (these are extra money allowances), family allowances and so on (see Chapter 5, Note 2). Gwyn's factory has had many 'wildcat' strikes, some called by the shop stewards, some by small groups of workers. Some of these strikes were about pay, some were about bad working conditions—the factory is badly planned, has not got enough windows and is too hot in summer. One strike was caused by the sacking of two men who became redundant. They had been given only one week's notice. Their mates struck in sympathy.

'The management don't think of us as human beings,' said Gwyn. 'How can a man feel safe, if his job can be taken from him with so little warning?'

There have also been strikes caused by quarrels between the unions. Although two-thirds of all union members belong to the eighteen biggest unions, there are altogether more than five hundred unions in Britain[1]. In Gwyn's factory, for example, there are workers from fifteen different unions.

Strikers during the miners' strike of 1972 try to persuade a lorry driver not to deliver coal.

Gwyn himself once caused a strike. There was a rush order for the Continent and Gwyn stayed behind after work to help load the lorries. The loaders went out on strike at once.

'Trying to make us redundant, are you, Taffy? You get back to your panel-beating.'

Gwyn and most of his mates do not enjoy striking, but they would like to be consulted on decisions which affect their work and their lives. For example, they would have liked to discuss with the management the advantages and disadvantages of the merger.

'You've got a work's committee, haven't you?' said the foreman.

'Well, what's the use of it?' said Gwyn. 'Whenever there's anything important to be decided, the management makes up its mind first and then tells us. The only *important* decision we've been asked to make lately is where the new wash-basins are to go, and what shape they're to be!'

IS ALL WELL WITH BRITISH BUSINESS? ANNE ASKS CHARLES SOME QUESTIONS

ANNE BLAKENEY: What's the first thing you're going to do, Charles, when you take over the business from your father next year?

CHARLES: Pay much more attention to market research. I've already got my eye on a good man for the job. Father has invested a lot of money in technical research but I still can't make him see how important market research is.

ANNE: I've never really understood market research. What is it, exactly?

CHARLES: It's simply finding out what customers want. It's no longer any good making the same old product year after year and saying: 'this is what you ought to want. It's well made. It's British. So come and buy it!' That used to be the tendency not so long ago, but nobody thinks like that today. We can't afford to. We've got too many competitors.

ANNE: Is it going to be a hard struggle, then?

CHARLES: Yes, because we—the British, I mean—earn our living by exporting manufactured goods[3]. The trouble is, we can't *export* without *importing* raw materials, and we have to buy these with dollars, marks and francs and so on. Then we have to try and sell our products in world markets.

ANNE: It seems to me that things'll never get any better.

CHARLES: They'll get better if we can increase our productivity, in other words produce more goods per worker. This'll mean that we'll be able to sell more abroad and keep more for ourselves at home. It's this 'growth' that so many people are looking for.

ANNE: But I thought our economy *was* growing.

CHARLES: It is, but not as fast as that of many other countries, and that's what matters.

ANNE: Why is our growth so poor?

CHARLES: Because we all want bigger profits and higher wages and shorter working hours. But to get all these things we need to be more efficient. To begin with, we ought to invest more money in new machinery. Some of our factories are still using machinery that's at least fifty years old, and in some industries the management is pretty old-fashioned too. Then there are the trade unions—they've got to bring themselves up-to-date. There are far too many unions, and no really effective way of stopping the absurd disagreements they so often have. Besides, the unions have no real control over their members now. About 90 per cent of all our strikes these days start unofficially, even if some of them are made official later. To put it bluntly, unless we increase our efficiency *all round*, we'll never increase our productivity.

ANNE: I'm not surprised that factory workers want shorter hours. How would you like to beat panels or turn screws hour after hour every day?

CHARLES: I wouldn't. I'd get bored, and I'd think only of my weekly wage packet.

ANNE: So naturally our workers are always on strike! They're bored, and they want more money to spend in their spare time!

CHARLES: It's a mistake to blame everything on strikes. Actually we have fewer strikes than many other countries.[11] We lose far more working hours through illness and through workers just taking a day off—like all industrial countries. No, what worries me is that there are far too many *unnecessary* disagreements between workers, trade unions and management. We haven't yet learned to work together as a team.

ANNE: Is that why so many of our industries are dying?

CHARLES: What do you mean, 'so many of our industries'? And what do you mean by 'dying'?

ANNE: That's the word you used the other day about coal-mining*, and

* Since the energy crisis, coal-mining has become an important industry (see p. 36).

the cotton textile industry.

CHARLES: Why do people get so upset about these industries? I suppose it's because they used to be our pride and strength. Well, they're not any more, and as far as I am concerned, the sooner people realise it the better. Then, all the money, labour and technical skill wasted on them could be put into expanding industries, like electronics, aero-engines, motor-cars, and so on. Some people wouldn't agree with me, of course.

ANNE: What about industries in other countries? Haven't they got the same sort of problems?

CHARLES: Yes, but they've had more practice at fighting for markets. That's why I'm in favour of Britain being a member of the Common Market. Industries inside the Common Market are *forced* to take notice of their competitors.

ANNE: Then you don't feel too hopeless about the future?

CHARLES: Of course I don't. We're a very inventive people and we have plenty of skilled workers. Besides, we still have our reputation for

RB 211 gas turbine engines.

honesty and fair dealing in business.

ANNE: Is that so important these days?

CHARLES: Indeed it is! Why do you think London is still the world's chief insurance market and such an important banking centre? The foreign money these services earn is one of our most important exports. In fact, without them we'd never be able to pay for our imports[3].

ANNE: How nice to hear you boast, Charlie! The English think it's in bad taste to boast, don't they? When foreigners ask you 'How are things?' and you answer, 'Not bad!' how are they to know that 'not bad!' often means 'first-class, thank you!'?

NOTES

(1) *Trade Unions*
There are over 500 trade unions but two-thirds of all trade unionists belong to the eighteen largest. The three largest unions are:

The Transport and General Workers Union	(1,785,496)
Amalgamated Union of Engineering Workers	(1,374,866)
National Union of General and Municipal Workers	(863,964)

(1974 figures)
But among the most powerful unions are the National Union of Mineworkers (261,171) and the National Union of Railwaymen (173,973). When either of these unions goes on strike, they can cause great harm to the economy of the country, and great misery to the public. On the other hand, they are underpaid compared with miners and railwaymen in most other Common Market countries. The miners are determined to force their way to the top of the wage scale in Britain. In 1974 they went on strike during the world's oil crisis and won large pay increases from the government.

(2) *The Trades Union Congress (T.U.C.)*
The T.U.C. was founded in 1868 and is a voluntary association of trade unions (i.e. no union can be forced to join the T.U.C.). In 1973–4, the numbers of unions in the T.U.C. was 109, with a total membership of 10,022,224. Some of the unions are themselves a federation of unions; for example, the Transport Union includes nine different unions.

The T.U.C. meets annually, has an elected council and a permanent general secretary. The government often asks the general secretary for advice and information, and the T.U.C. often gives the government unasked-for advice. In 1976 it cooperated closely with the Labour Government (see page 87, Note 9). The T.U.C. is very jealous of its rights and dislikes interference of any kind from the government or anyone else. In the same way unions are not always willing to accept advice from the T.U.C.—unless they agree with it. The T.U.C. has no authority (i.e. power) over the unions.

(3) *Britain's position in the world as a trading country*
Britain is the world's fourth largest exporter of manufactured goods (after West Germany, USA and Japan). But in the early and mid-1970s she imported far more goods than she exported, increasing the National Debt and seriously damaging home industries. Some factories were forced to close down or make many of their workers redundant. The effect on inflation was serious.

Britain has one of the largest merchant fleets. British ship-building is going through a bad time, but is still amongst the most important in the world.

Britain is one of the world's most important manufacturers of aircraft frames, complete aircraft, and, above all, aero-engines (Rolls Royce).

Britain is the largest importer of wheat, butter, tobacco; the second largest importer of wool (after Japan); and the third largest importer of citrus fruits, that is, oranges, lemons, etc. (after W. Germany and France).

Amongst Britain's most important exports are the services which she sells (i.e. shipping, banking, insurance, tourism, etc.). These 'invisible earnings', as they are often called, are second only to those of the USA. Many foreign insurance companies re-insure in Britain, especially with Lloyds, the most famous insurance association in the world. London is the centre of the diamond and gold trades and a great world market for all kinds of goods.

North Sea Oil: Britain's oil fields in the North Sea, so some experts say, will provide her with all the oil she needs by 1980. Others say it will take longer. Some experts say it will make England rich again. Others are doubtful.

(4) *The Confederation of British Industry (C.B.I.)*
The organisation which represents employers in private industry. It consults with the trade unions and gives advice to the government.

(5) *Bank of England*
The state bank, which lends and borrows money for the government, handles production of notes and currency, manages the national debt and is in control of the nation's gold reserve. It was founded not long after the revolution of 1688 and is generally regarded as the world's most famous bank. A common expression is: 'as safe as the Bank of England'.

(6) *Stock Exchange*
The institution in the City where stocks and shares are bought and sold.

(7) *Food*

Britain grows about half the food she needs (some claim more), but only 1·8 per cent of her total workforce work full-time on farms. This is the lowest percentage in the world. British agriculture is highly mechanised and has one of the highest tractor densities in the world.

(8) *Tourism*

Foreign tourism is growing twice as fast in Britain as in the world generally. It earns more U.S. dollars than any other single industry.

(9) *Inflation* (Increase in prices—decrease in the value of money)

General increase in consumer prices, 1970–74

Denmark	41·6%	Sweden	31·7%
Japan	52%	Norway	32·5%
France	35·8%	Italy	43·5%
Netherlands	36·4%	Britain	48·7%

In the early and mid-1970s wages rose faster than prices, partly as a result of successful strikes. This was one of the most serious causes of inflation. 'Inflation' was a word on everybody's lips. But because of higher wages, the standard of living did not drop as much as people expected.

(10) *The Introduction of Decimal Currency*

On 15 February 1971 the new decimal currency came into use in Britain. Shillings disappeared and the pound is now divided into 100 new pence. There are six new coins, but the pound note and the five pound note remain the same.

This was the first step which Britain took towards complete metrication. At the present time the metrication of weights and measures is taking place gradually. Already much of British industry has 'gone metric', but elsewhere, such as in shops, measurements are still given in inches, feet and yards as well as in centimetres and metres. The same is true of weights. For some time now temperatures have been given both according to the Centigrade scale and the Fahrenheit scale.

(11) *International comparison of the effect of strikes: number of working days lost*

	1964	1973
United States	22,900,000	27,000,918
UK	2,277,000	7,197,000
Australia	911,358	2,634,700
Belgium	443,835	871,872
Netherlands	43,862	583,783
West Germany		563,051
Sweden	34,000	11,802
Spain	141,153	1,081,158
France	2,496,791	3,914,598
Italy	13,088,609	23,419,285

(12)

Number of private cars, television sets and telephones per thousand people

*1971 figure

(13) *Distribution of personal income in Britain 1969–70*

| Earnings in a year | Number of people | |
	before tax	after tax
(Figures from Inland Revenue)		
under £1,000	8,649,000	10,723,000
£1,000–£1,999	10,418,000	9,732,000
£2,000–£2,999	1,864,000	903,000
£3,000–£4,999	548,000	299,000
£5,000–£9,999	205,000	76,000
£10,000 or over	50,000	1,000

QUESTIONS

(1) What are the advantages and disadvantages of belonging to a trade union? Do unions benefit the country as well as the workers?

(2) It has been suggested recently that the state should not pay supplementary benefits to the families of strikers. Do you agree?

(3) Charles thinks that workers, unions and management ought to work together. Is he being too optimistic?

(4) There are more than five hundred unions in Britain. Are there too many? How many are there in your country?

FURTHER READING

Sillitoe, A. F.   Britain in Figures
McCarthy, W. E. J.   Trade Unions

The statue of Justice is at the top of the Old Bailey, the Central Criminal Court.

The opening of a new session of the Law Courts is marked by a special service at Westminster Abbey. Then the judges walk in procession to the House of Lords.

7
Policemen and
Justice

THE POLICE AND THE GENERAL PUBLIC

How do the police get on with the general public in Britain? It is claimed by some people that the police have prejudices against students and against coloured immigrants. A short time ago, Leonard Townsend led a discussion on the problem with a Chief Inspector of Police, Jeremy Martin, and a left-wing militant student, Sandy Piggott.

LEONARD TOWNSEND: We in Britain like to think that the relationship between the police and the British public is better than in most other countries[1]. Sandy Piggott, I understand that you have strong feelings about the police?

SANDY PIGGOTT: I certainly have! The police are just tools of the government. The government use the police to destroy political freedom.

CHIEF INSPECTOR: This is, of course, complete nonsense. No government minister, or local councillor, has the authority to order the police to arrest anybody for any crime whatsoever, political or otherwise[2]. It is the police themselves who decide whether a person should be arrested or not.

S.P: But the police arrest students who demonstrate!

C.I: Only if they cause a disturbance.

L.T: You're not against demonstrations, then, Inspector?

C.I: Certainly not. The law is perfectly clear on this point. Demonstrations are lawful as long as there is no disturbance of the peace.

The right to demonstrate is an important British freedom.

s.p: What do you mean by 'disturbance of the peace', Inspector?

c.i: It's clear, isn't it? Trying to break into buildings, stopping people going about their lawful business, hitting policemen . . . .

s.p: And what about policemen who hit demonstrators?

c.i: It is extremely regrettable. But policemen are not above the law. If you can prove that a policeman has used unnecessary force, or caused injury, you can take him to court.

s.p: You admit, then, that the police are violent!

c.i: I have admitted nothing. But you seem to forget that policemen are human beings like everybody else. Can you blame them if they don't like being kicked or scratched or hit in the face? I think it's surprising how rarely they lose their tempers.

l.t: I'm sure that many people would agree with you, Inspector, but it is not only young people who claim that the police are sometimes too rough with demonstrators.

c.i: It depends on what you mean by 'rough'. We've never yet used water cannon, or tear gas, and, to my knowledge, we've never used our truncheons, either.*

l.t: Jeremy Martin, you've continued to take part in demonstrations since leaving university. What are your feelings about the police?

j.m: I'm rather sorry for them. It's their job to enforce the law as it is, and I think that on the whole they do it with moderation. I've taken part in demonstrations in other countries, so I can make comparisons.

l.t: Clearly you and Sandy Piggott don't agree then.

j.m: No we don't! Sandy and his friends represent only a very small minority of students in this country, yet they're doing more than anyone else to make students unpopular. It's because of what they're doing that people are asking for tougher action from the police. Too many people are becoming obsessed with law and order when they ought to be thinking of more important things. And it's partly Sandy Piggott's fault.

s.p: Rubbish! It's the fault of *your* bourgeois society!

l.t: Have you *no* criticisms of the police, then, Jeremy Martin?

j.m: Oh, certainly I've got criticisms of the police! To begin with, I don't think enough policemen try to understand young people. I've been spoken to roughly just because I've got long hair.

l.t: Inspector?

* The Inspector is not including the Ulster Constabulary, which is an entirely separate police force. (see p. 42).

c.i: Policemen have prejudices like everybody else. But it's part of police training to discourage these prejudices.

j.m: I've heard that policemen spend more time in learning how to drill than in learning about social problems. What do they really know about the colour problem, for example? I've got West Indian friends who feel, rightly or wrongly, that the police are prejudiced against coloured immigrants.

c.i: This is a very difficult problem, I agree, but I honestly believe that some coloured immigrants have stronger prejudices against the police than the police have against them.

j.m: But wouldn't you admit, Inspector, that the police know very little about the background of the coloured community? That they know practically nothing about their customs, their religions, their past history, and so on?

c.i: They don't know enough, I agree, but doesn't this sort of thing always happen when minority groups settle in a new country? After all, the Irish didn't have an easy time when they first came to Britain.

l.t: What is being done, Inspector, to improve relations between the police and the coloured community?

c.i: A lot! We've got special officers now whose job it is to keep in touch with the immigrant leaders. They listen to complaints, give advice and learn a great deal at the same time. But you know, Mr Townsend, students and immigrants aren't the only people the police have to deal with!

s.p: You mean the old ladies and little children they help across the road![3]

c.i: No, I mean the real criminals. We might catch a few more of them if we didn't have to send so many men to your demonstrations.

THE POLICE, FIRE-ARMS AND THE DEATH PENALTY

'Look at this!' said Carlos, pointing to his newspaper. ' "Two policemen shot down by robbers in front of bank!" This sort of thing wouldn't happen so often if your policemen were armed.'

'I think it would probably happen more often,' said Charles. 'Criminals tend to shoot first when they know that policemen have guns. We don't want any gun battles in our streets.'

The British police are given guns only when they are hunting dangerous criminals or terrorists, and even then only when it is known that these persons have fire-arms[4] and are likely to use them. Few people want the police to be armed, and very few policemen would like to carry guns, although a great many of them would like to see the death penalty for murder re-introduced[5].

'They think that the fear of being hanged would discourage criminals from using extreme violence,' said Charles, 'and judging from opinion polls, the general public thinks the same.'

'Well, Parliament, for once, was sensible enough not to give way to public opinion!' said Anne. 'Countries which have abolished the death penalty haven't found that the number of murders has increased.'

'But we've got to do something about violent crime especially about terrorism,' said Charles.

'Plenty of other countries have terrorists,' Anne said. 'I'd have thought there was still less violence in Britain than in most other places. I certainly don't think that bringing back hanging would cure terrorism. It would just make martyrs. Anyway, isn't hanging itself a form of violence?'

THE POLICE MAKE AN ARREST

One Sunday evening a police sergeant and a constable knocked at the door of number 10 Royal Row.

'Mr Williams?' said the sergeant. 'We have reason to believe that there is stolen property in this house. We'd like to see your son, Jim.'

Gwyn looked at the policeman suspiciously.

'What's he done?'

'The doorstep isn't a good place to talk, is it sir?' said the sergeant. 'May we come inside?'

Gwyn hesitated. Then he said: 'Have you got a warrant?'

'As a matter of fact, we have, sir,' said the sergeant.

He showed Gwyn a document signed by the local magistrate (see p. 121) which gave him the right to enter the Williams' house and search it. Without this warrant the police could enter the house only if Gwyn 'invited' them in.

The sergeant and the constable followed Gwyn into the sitting-room. Jim was there.

Jim looked at the policemen, then at his father.

'You don't have to say anything, son,' said Gwyn. 'But I'd like to know what you've been up to.'

Gwyn knew the law. He knew that the police could not use threats or force to make his son talk, and that they could not arrest him unless they had fairly strong evidence that he had committed a crime. They could only 'invite' him to go with them to the police station for questioning and, once at the station, they could not keep him there unless they could charge him with a crime.

The police have to bring prisoners before the court as soon as possible, usually within twenty-four hours. No prison without trial is one of the most important rights that an Englishman has. It dates from the Habeus Corpus Act of 1679. 'Habeus Corpus' is the Latin for 'You shall produce the body', in other words, the body of the prisoner must be brought before the court. The act of 1679 is one of the cornerstones of British justice.

'I'm not saying anything!' replied Jim.

'Listen, son!' said Gwyn. 'If you're hiding anything in this house, go and get it. I'm not having the police turn my cupboards inside out.'

Jim went upstairs and came back a moment later with five cigarette lighters. He was arrested at once.

'It's those friends of his!' said Mary.

'Yes, officer,' said Gwyn. 'You'd better go and have a talk with Rob Milligan and his boys!'

The sergeant said nothing. Nor did Jim. He was taken out to the police car and driven straight to the local police station.

'Caution him!' the sergeant told the constable as soon as they arrived. The constable took out his notebook.

'Do you wish to say anything?' he said to Jim. 'You are not obliged to say anything unless you wish to do so. But whatever you say will be taken down in writing and may be given in evidence.'

These are the words which every policeman must use before questioning a person accused of a crime. This 'caution' tells the accused quite clearly that the police cannot *force* him to convict himself by what he says.

The constable told Jim to sit down.

'Now then, where were you at 5.25 on Thursday evening?'

'I'm not talking—copper!'

'All right!' said the constable calmly. 'I'll wait. But it'll help you if you tell the truth.'

At last Jim agreed to talk. In other words, he agreed to make a

Two important aspects of police work — a policeman ('bobby') accompanies a demonstration, and a C.I.D. man checks the records.

statement, in which he admitted that he knew the cigarette lighters had been stolen. He also told the constable exactly when and where Rob Milligan had given him the lighters.

After writing down Jim's statement, the constable read it back to him.

'Anything else you want to say?'

'Nothing that you'd like to hear!' said Jim.

The constable handed him a pen.

'Write this down,' he said.

Jim wrote: 'I have read the above statement and have been told that I can correct, alter (change), or add anything I wish. This statement is true. I have made it of my own free will.'

Every written statement must finish with these words, preferably written in the accused person's own handwriting.

'Sign it,' said the constable.

Jim signed. He was then charged with having 'received stolen goods'.

MAGISTRATES' COURTS

The morning after his night in the police cells, Jim Williams was brought before the local magistrate. So was Rob Milligan.

Every district has a magistrates' court. Most magistrates, or Justices of the Peace, as they are also called (J.P. for short), have had little training in law and receive no salary. They are usually men or women who are well known and respected in the district, who accept this part-time job for the honour of it, or from a sense of duty. They are drawn from all social backgrounds. Very few are paid professionals.

Magistrates can only try people for minor, i.e. not very serious, offences. They cannot give prison sentences totalling more than twelve months. They cannot order fines of more than £400 for one offence. If, after hearing all the evidence, they decide that the crime is a serious one, they must send the accused for trial in a higher court.

In Jim Williams' case, the magistrate found him guilty of having received stolen goods. But because of his age, and since it was his first offence, the magistrate was not severe. He put him on probation for twelve months, which meant that Jim had to report once a week to a probation officer, whose job it was to help and advise him and discourage him from committing further crimes.

Rob Milligan's case was very different. When stealing the cigarette lighters he had hit the shopkeeper over the head. He had also been in the courts twice before for causing a disturbance. The magistrate had no power to try Rob for such a serious offence as 'robbery with violence'. Instead, he ordered him to be kept in prison until he could be sent for trial to the higher court.

TRIAL BY JURY

In all large towns there is at least one Crown Court (part of the High Court) where trials are held more or less continuously. The most serious offences are dealt with by High Court judges from London. Other serious offences are dealt with by circuit (travelling) judges. In London, however, prisoners accused of serious offences are tried at the Old Bailey, the Central Criminal Court which has been the scene of some of Britain's most famous murder trials. The Old Bailey has many courts, and it was in one of these that Rob Milligan's trial was held.

All criminal trials in the Crown Courts and at the Old Bailey are held before a judge and jury[6]. The beginnings of the jury system can be found in the eleventh century, and it became the basis of British justice. The jury represents the people, and it is the jury, not the judge, which decides whether an accused person is guilty or not.

A British jury is composed of twelve members. Any householder — Gwyn and Mary Williams, Sir Eric, the Macdonalds — can be ordered to serve on a jury, and they cannot refuse unless they have a very good reason.

During Rob's trial the jury sat in silence and listened to all the evidence. They were not allowed to ask any questions. At the end of the trial they listened carefully to the summing-up of the judge, the speech in which he reminded them of all the most important arguments put forward by the lawyer prosecuting Rob, and by the lawyer defending him.

When the judge had finished his summing-up, the jury retired to the jury room where they stayed—locked in—until they had reached their verdict, or decision, which had to be either 'guilty' or 'not guilty'. In a British court of law the accused is always innocent until he is proved guilty, so the jury at Rob's trial had to be absolutely sure that he had hit the shopkeeper on the head before they could return a verdict of guilty. Their verdict *was* 'guilty' and the judge sentenced Rob to two years in prison[6].

The lawyer who had defended Rob was a distinguished barrister.[7] He had been suggested by the solicitor to whom Rob's father had gone for advice. The entire cost of Rob's defence was paid for by the state, since the Milligan family were too poor to pay for it themselves. Everyone in Britain has the right to be defended free of cost if he cannot afford the lawyer's fees, and he has the right to employ the best barrister he can find. If he cannot find a lawyer himself the court will find one for him.

AN OPINION ON BRITISH JUSTICE

Elizabeth Townsend knows Rob Milligan and his family. One day during his case she and Leonard began talking about the British system of justice.

'A lot of English people think our system is one of the best in the world,' she said. 'Is that just because they're English?'

'In many cases, yes,' Leonard replied, 'because most of them don't know much about the systems in other countries, so they're not really in a position to judge. I mean, they can judge whether the English system is good or bad, but they can't or shouldn't compare it with something they know nothing about.'

'Don't you think that most people, whatever their nationality, think that their own system is the best?'

'Not necessarily. Some foreigners admire the British police and system of justice.'

'But what do you yourself think?'

'Well, if I were accused of a crime, I'd have confidence in the judge and jury if I were tried in England—or Scotland. Of course, judges and juries sometimes make mistakes, but that only happens rarely. When it does happen, it's generally in favour of the accused. Besides, there are so many safeguards. For example, the prosecution must produce all the known facts, even facts which favour the accused. Nothing can be hidden.'

'What about our judges?'

'I think the great majority of them are decent, humane people. And certainly they're all honest. They really do try to treat every prisoner as equal before the law, whatever his race, nationality or religion. But I think some of them are too old, which makes it difficult for them to understand the problems of today.'

Judges are not controlled in any way by the government. They are appointed by the Lord High Chancellor, who is himself a lawyer and a member of the government. All judges have had a distinguished record as barristers.

'I think that *this* is the most important thing about British justice,' said Leonard. 'Our judges are completely non-political. They remain in office however often the government changes.'

NOTES
(1) Opinion Research Centre carried out a survey in December 1969, for *The Sunday Times*, with a sample of 930 adults. They found that 86 per cent of the population respect and admire policemen a great deal, 95 per cent consider them helpful, 93 per cent friendly, 95 per cent honest, 93 per cent fair. 89 per cent of the 16–24 year old age group agree that policemen are usually polite.

(2) There are forty-one police forces in Britain, each employed and paid by local authorities. They get half their money from the local rates and half from the Treasury. The forces are completely independent of one another, but they help each other. Each force has its C.I.D. — Criminal Investigation Department (investigate means to 'inquire' or 'examine').

The London Police force, called the Metropolitan Police, is *not* controlled by the local authority. It is responsible to the Home Secretary, and its chief officers are appointed by the government. But once appointed these officers cannot easily be dismissed, and they take their decisions without interference from ministers. 'Scotland Yard', the famous C.I.D. of the Metropolitan Police, is so called because the headquarters of the Metropolitan Police used to be in Scotland Yard, near Whitehall. Provincial police forces sometimes ask Scotland Yard C.I.D. for help in cases of serious crime.

N.B. If in trouble, or if you have witnessed a crime, go to the nearest telephone and dial 999. You will be put through immediately to the Post Office, who will ask you which service you want — Police, Fire Brigade or Ambulance. The policemen, firemen or an ambulance will arrive within a few minutes.

(3) *The Police and Traffic*
There are no special traffic police in Britain. The British police complain that they have to spend far too much time controlling the traffic and dealing with traffic offences. This, they say, damages their relationship with the public.
Traffic Wardens
Traffic wardens were first introduced in 1960. In 1975 there were about 6,000 in England and Wales. They deal with minor traffic offences, like parking in the wrong place, or without lights; they report car owners who do not have a licence; they supervise school children crossing roads.

(4) *Fire-arm Laws*

Anyone who wants to own a gun, even a shot-gun (a gun for shooting birds or rabbits) must get a fire-arm certificate from the police. Except in the case of shot-guns, very few certificates are given.

(5) *The Death Penalty*

Punishment by death was abolished for a trial period of five years in 1965. In December 1969 the Labour Home Secretary introduced a bill abolishing the death penalty permanently. There was a 'free vote' in Parliament, in which each member was free to vote according to his conscience and not according to party orders. The bill was passed by 343 votes to 185.

A motion calling for the reintroduction of the death penalty for terrorists was debated in Parliament in December 1975 but it was rejected.

(6) *The Jury and the Verdict*

Since the accused is considered to be innocent until he is proved guilty, the prosecution must *prove* his guilt; the defence does not have to prove his innocence. If there is doubt in the minds of the jury, the verdict must be 'not guilty'. In Scottish law, a jury may return a verdict of 'not proven' (not proved), but even then the verdict is final and a person may not be tried twice for the same crime. Until 1966 in England and Wales all the members of the jury had to be in agreement. Now, at least ten of the twelve jury members must agree before a verdict can be given. In Scotland, the number is nine. If the jury is too divided, there must be a new trial with a new jury.

(7) *Lawyers*

There are two kinds of lawyers:

Solicitors advise citizens on all questions of law and prepare cases for barristers.

Barristers speak in law courts. As 'counsel for the prosecution' a barrister will try to prove the accused person's guilt. As 'counsel for the defence' he will defend the accused.

(8) *British Criminal Law*

There are two forms, common law and statute law. Common law is made up of general customs, some of which have been regarded as the laws in the land for centuries. Common law has grown up slowly through the ages, like the British Constitution. It is sometimes called 'unwritten law'. However, much of common law has become statute law, that is to say, it has been put down in writing by Acts of Parliament. Murder still belongs to common law, while attempts to murder have become statute law.

(9) *Courts of Appeal*

In law 'to appeal' is to ask a higher court to change the judgement already given by a lower court. Criminals have the right to appeal against their sentences to the Court of Appeal. If the appeal is refused there can be a final appeal to the House of Lords, but this rarely happens.

(10) *Juvenile Courts* (Courts for young offenders under seventeen)

The aim of these courts is not to punish but to correct and give helpful advice. Young offenders may be sent to special 'approved' schools. These are educational institutions, housed in open buildings. Some come under the local education authorities and all have to be approved by the Home Office. The character of the schools, and the type of technical education given in each, varies, but the atmosphere is very different from that found in the old reform

Emergency calls

These calls are free; lift receiver and listen for dial tone (continuous purring)

dial **999**   and ask operator for

FIRE, POLICE OR AMBULANCE

this telephone is

CO 400   Dd. 681338 84 (7174)

If you are ever in trouble dial 999. The instructions are clear, and appear in every telephone box.

Traffic wardens are easy to recognise because of their uniforms.

A sculpture class at an approved school— an institution which caters for young offenders.

schools and industrial schools, which were replaced by the approved schools in 1933 by Act of Parliament.

Sociologists claim that teenage violence in the cities is caused partly by boredom. There are not enough opportunities for 'lawful' adventure. There are not enough good youth clubs and too few imaginative youth leaders. One or two adventure clubs have now been started in the East End of London. They organise trips to interesting places and encourage young people to make things.

QUESTIONS

(1) Do students deserve their unpopularity?

(2) Do you think that the police force should be armed?

(3) It is generally thought that a majority of the British are in favour of the death penalty, and yet Parliament has abolished it. What do you think about this situation?

(4) Magistrates have little training in the law. What are the advantages and the disadvantages of this? Do you think they should all be professionals?

(5) Young offenders are often put on probation or sent to approved schools. Many people think the problem needs more radical and imaginative solutions. What would you do with young criminals?

FURTHER READING

Jenkins, R.   The Lawbreakers *(Connexions)*
Street, H.   Freedom, the Individual and the Law
Fuller, L.   The Anatomy of the Law
Whittaker, B.   The Police
Cecil, H.   Friends at Court (F)

There is a powerful contrast between this ultra-modern church and thirteenth-century Wells Cathedral.

8

How the British Worship

There is complete religious freedom in Britain. Religion has always played an important part in the national way of life and this is still true today, though changes are taking place and will continue to do so.

THE CHURCH OF ENGLAND

The Archbishop of Canterbury is the Primate of all England, that is to say, he is the spiritual leader of the Church of England. After him, the Archbishop of York is called the Primate of England and under these two archbishops come a number of bishops. England is divided into forty-two districts called dioceses, each with a bishop in charge and a cathedral as the central church. A diocese is divided into smaller districts called parishes. These vary in size, a large town having a number of parishes and a village being a single parish. Each parish is in the care of a priest, who is called either a vicar or a rector. A vicar with a large parish may have an assistant priest called a curate to help him.

The Church of England (or the Anglican Church) is the 'national' church in England, established by law[1]. In spite of this, it runs its own affairs and does not receive any money from the state since it owns stocks and shares and a great deal of land and other properties.

Many people would say that the Church of England today is both Protestant and Catholic; there is certainly a great variety of beliefs and practices within the Church. A look at some church notice-boards might confuse anyone unfamiliar with the differences between 'high church' and 'low church'. A look inside the churches would probably add to the confusion. A visitor entering a high church at, say, ten o'clock on a Sunday morning might find a high (sung) mass in progress and think he had entered a Roman Catholic church (the name Anglo-Catholic is sometimes used for this kind of church). The church would probably be highly decorated, the priests would be wearing various kinds of robes, people would light candles to the Virgin Mary and go to the priests for confession. By contrast, a low church service would be as simple as possible; there would be no ceremony, no candles, no private confessions and the church would look rather bare. It would seem to have more in common with the nonconformist churches[2]. Between these two extremes there are churches with more or less ceremony, depending mainly on the views of the vicar in charge. Some Anglican priests have broken away from tradition to the extent that in some services they introduce new religious songs, composed by young people who accompany them on guitars in the church. They also use the church as a place where people can discuss the problems of everyday life; in other words, these priests want the church to become a meeting place in a wider sense, not simply for the more traditional type of religious service.

THE BLAKENEYS GO TO CHURCH

In the little town near Blakeney Hall there are seven different Christian churches—an Anglican church (Church of England), a Catholic church, a Methodist church, a Congregational chapel, a Baptist chapel, a Quaker meeting-house, and a Salvation Army hall. There are also people who belong to other quite separate religious groups, non-Christian as well as Christian. There are about 100 Jews, ten Muslims and two or three Hindus[3].

Carlos, who was spending a week at Blakeney Hall, was astonished.

'What a pity there's not as much variety in English cooking as there is in English religions!' he said.

The Blakeneys are members of the Church of England and go to church every Sunday morning. They sit in an ancient oak pew which has belonged to the Blakeney family for more than 400 years.

It was a fine Sunday morning in autumn. As Hester and Sir Eric reached the door of the little Norman church, the Blandfords arrived from the opposite direction. Phyllis Blandford was wearing a white hat with a large bunch of artificial fruit pinned to it.

'I do wish *you* would wear a hat, Hester!' said Sir Eric. 'You're the only one who doesn't.'

They waited for the Blandfords.

'Well, Eric,' said George Blandford. 'I suppose you'll be out in the woods with your gun this afternoon.'

'Yes,' replied Sir Eric. 'Like to join me?'

The congregation stood up as the small choir appeared from the back of the church and walked slowly forward to take their places at the front. There were five little boys, four women and four men, followed by the vicar.

'Hymn 643,' he said.

It was Sir Eric's favourite hymn, 'Onward Christian Soldiers, marching as to war'.

'Not so loud, Eric!' said Hester. 'You're singing out of tune!'

They knelt to say the Lord's Prayer. They sang a psalm. They listened to a passage from the Old Testament, read by George Blandford. Then they sang another psalm and listened to a reading from the New Testament, read by the vicar. They stood to say the Creed, their declaration of faith: 'I believe in God the Father Almighty, Maker of Heaven and Earth, and in Jesus Christ, His only Son our Lord....' More prayers, another hymn—and it was time for the sermon. The vicar climbed into the pulpit.

Sir Eric's eyes closed. The Reverend Elliot Willmott's sermons were usually long. Hester pinched him.

'Remember last Sunday!' she whispered. 'You snored!'

Sir Eric stayed awake with an effort, and thought about the afternoon's shoot. The sun shone through the ancient stained-glass windows. What luck that the weather was good! At last the sermon was over. Another hymn, and the final blessing—and they were out in the sunshine once more.

The women stopped to chat for a few minutes, and the vicar joined them. Raymond and Sir Eric made plans for the afternoon's sport. Then they all went home to their Sunday lunch.

Charles and Anne had driven down for the weekend. Charles had spent the Sunday morning playing golf with Carlos.

'I'm sure your father would rather have played golf with you both,' said Anne. 'Going to church is just a social occasion for him and rather a boring one, I suspect.'

'True,' said Charles. 'But it's always been a tradition of the Blakeneys to uphold and respect the established Church! Besides, Father really minds what people here think about him. Some of them would be terribly shocked if he played golf instead of going to church.'

THE CHURCH OF SCOTLAND

The Presbyterian Church is the established Church of Scotland. It is completely separate from the Anglican Church, has its own organisation with a 'Moderator' as the elected leader of the church assembly, and appoints its own ministers. Presbyterianism is a severe form of Protestantism, founded in the sixteenth century and following the teaching of the great French reformer, Calvin. John Knox, a Roman Catholic priest who was converted to Protestantism, established Presbyterianism in Scotland and the majority of Presbyterians in England are Scots or descendants of Scots who have gone to live south of the border.

THE MACDONALDS DO NOT GO TO CHURCH

Last summer, during a Scottish tour, Peggy and Ian spent a few days with Ian's uncle, Angus Macdonald, who lives with his wife in a lonely Highland cottage. Uncle Angus did not give them a very warm welcome, for, being a strict Presbyterian, he was disappointed that his nephew had married a Roman Catholic.

On Sunday morning Uncle Angus said to Ian: 'Will *you* be coming to the kirk with us, Ian?' ('kirk' is the Scottish word for church).

'Well, no, if you don't mind, Uncle,' Ian replied. 'But we'll walk down to the village with you.'

They walked in silence down the mountainside to the grey stone kirk by the loch. Uncle Angus and his wife joined the procession of solemn-faced people who were already entering the bare little church. The minister arrived, dressed all in black.

'Ugh!' said Peggy, when the doors were closed. 'I'm glad I'm not a Presbyterian. It's all so cold and unfriendly!'

'Well, some Presbyterians think that your services are *too* friendly,' said Ian. 'Like a sort of theatrical show! In fact, really strict Presbyterians, like Uncle Angus, think that Catholic services—even Church of England services—are ungodly.'

*Religion in the open air
—two different
traditions.*

133

Lunch was solemn and silent, but afterwards Peggy said brightly: 'Why don't we all go for a sight-seeing trip down the glen?'

Uncle Angus looked at her in astonishment.

'On the Lord's Day?' he asked.

Then without another word he sat down at the table, opened the big family Bible and began to read. Ian and Peggy crept upstairs to their room.

'Let's have a little music to cheer us up!' said Peggy.

She turned on her transistor radio. A woman's voice was singing 'Won't you come dancing with me!'

'Turn it down!' Ian said urgently.

Finally Ian and Peggy decided that they could stand it no longer. Without telling Uncle Angus they went for a drive. They did not get very far, however, because the ferry across the loch was not running. In some parts of the Highlands the ferries still do not run on Sundays, in spite of the heavy tourist traffic.

Not many Scottish Presbyterians are so strict or intolerant as Uncle Angus. In certain areas of Scotland there is a large percentage of Roman Catholics[4] and where Catholics and Presbyterians live together there is a good relationship. But the Church of Scotland is powerful and its influence tends to be rather puritanical.

The word 'puritan' dates from the sixteenth century when a small group of Protestant nonconformists tried to 'purify' the Church of England of all 'popish' or Roman Catholic influence. These Puritans believed that all wordly pleasures were ungodly. In the seventeenth century, disgusted by the wickedness of the *Old* World, a small band of them sailed away to found a new, 'godly' society in the still uninfected (pure) wilderness of the *New* World. The Puritans who sailed from Plymouth to New England in the Mayflower in 1620 were among the founders of modern America.

Puritanism remained, and still remains, strong on both sides of the Atlantic, especially among some of the nonconformists. The English complain that Sunday in Scotland is dull, but to most visitors from other countries Sunday in England is hardly less dull. Although it has been possible for some years to go to the cinema on Sunday evenings, there are few other entertainments on a Sunday. Sunday cricket (see p. 185) has at last been allowed, but professional football on Sundays is still a subject of discussion. Even people who have no religious objections to sport on Sunday simply want to keep one day of the week as a day of peace and quiet.

THE CHURCHES AND THE MODERN WORLD

Here is an extract from a television discussion, led by Leonard Townsend. Taking part are The Reverend Mervyn Porter of the Church of England; Penny Martin, a Roman Catholic; Jeremy Martin, an agnostic.

JEREMY MARTIN: If you ask the average Englishman what his religion is he'll most likely say, 'Well, C. of E., I suppose.' Then ask him how often he goes to church!

LEONARD TOWNSEND: According to figures which I have here, about 65 per cent of British couples get married in a church. More than 90 per cent of those who die get a Christian funeral, but less than 20 per cent go regularly to church. Mervyn Porter?

MERVYN PORTER: We oughtn't to judge a person's attitude to religion by how often he goes to church. Besides, I've got figures which show that more books and articles are being written about religion today than ever before—which shows that there must be a market for them—which suggests that the *interest* in religion is greater than ever before!

J.M: There's certainly an interest in religion, but is it helping people to love one another? Just take a look round the world! You don't have to look further than Northern Ireland, actually.

M.P: Northern Ireland isn't a good example, but on the other hand, what's happening in Ireland is helping to bring the churches over here closer together. In Britain today priests and ministers from all denominations, Catholic and Protestant, meet regularly to discuss ways of encouraging Christian unity. They even preach in each other's churches[5].

L.T: Roman Catholicism is a minority religion in Britain. Yet according to my figures the number of Catholics in this country has more than doubled during the last twenty-five years. This is a remarkable increase. There are now six million Catholics in Britain. Penny Martin, you recently became a Catholic. Can you tell us why?

PENNY MARTIN: I find the discipline of the Catholic Church a great comfort, and I like its ceremonies.

L.T: But aren't Catholics, too, questioning the authority of their leaders on certain questions, like the marriage of priests, for example?

P.M: Yes, naturally there are some things one must question. But doubts of this sort don't shake my faith.

L.T: Mervyn Porter?

M.P: I can understand how Penny feels. Roman Catholics are absolutely certain that their Church is the One Church, and this is a great strength to them. I'm sure Penny also finds it very reassuring to know that she will get the same kind of service in whatever part of the country—or the world—she happens to be. Who the priest is doesn't matter. Anglicans tend to go to church if they like their vicar, and to stay away if they don't.

L.T: Are you suggesting that this freedom is a disadvantage to the Church of England?

M.P: Yes and no. The fact that Anglican priests can and do disagree about so many things makes it more difficult for Anglicans to have the same absolute certainty in their faith that Catholics have. But I believe that this freedom does help Anglican priests to talk to people—including non-believers and doubters like Jeremy!

L.T: Penny mentioned the attraction of ceremony, or ritual. You are a low church man. Do you disapprove of ritual?

M.P: Not if it helps people to come closer to God. The trouble is, I think, that some people go to church out of habit to perform certain rituals. When this happens the ritual becomes meaningless.

L.T: What do you consider should be the first duty of a priest?

M.P: The first duty of a priest is the 'cure, or care, of souls'. But I personally don't think you can separate spiritual welfare from social welfare. In other words, I feel that I am doing more for the souls of a slum family if I find them a better house than if I persuade them to come to my church.

J.M: Doesn't that make the Church rather like a charitable organisation or a branch of the welfare state?

M.P: Social welfare has always been a tradition of the Church. In fact, most charities began through the Church. But of course the Church is much more than a charity. People who are worried by problems of conscience don't usually go to a social worker. They go to a priest.

J.M: I wouldn't go to a priest! If I went to anyone, I'd go to a friend. Problems of that sort are private and personal.

P.M: And what about people who haven't got friends?

L.T: Why are you so critical of the churches, Jeremy?

J.M: Because they have all the faults of the society of which they are part. They are authoritarian, too concerned with dogma, and not enough with people. The whole history of the Churches, Protestant and Catholic, is one of intolerance and cruelty. Besides, you can't expect the young people of today to accept blindly biblical stories which don't make any sense in the light of modern knowledge. If the Christian Church wants to survive it's got to bring itself up-to-date. It's got to make an effort to keep in touch with people. I don't know whether God exists or not, but if he does, I'm sure he doesn't really mind whether people are Christian, Hindu, Moslem or Buddhist as long as they are sincere.

M.P: I sympathise with Jeremy, but he certainly has got a rather old-fashioned view of the Christian faith. The Churches are doing a great deal of rethinking about the nature of God. They are trying to get closer to ordinary people and to help them with their problems, whatever their religious beliefs. 'Make love not war!' Isn't that what many young people say today? Well, if you take 'love' in the true sense of the word, that is what the Churches are trying to do.

L.T: Do you feel that the Church still has an important part to play in solving world problems? Penny?

P.M: Yes, I do. But I think that faith is more important than any political or social influence that the Church may have.

L.T: Jeremy?

J.M: Faith by itself isn't going to solve any problems. In any case, in the past the Church has often created more problems than it's solved. Social reforms have mostly come from the efforts of individual people—and not just Christians. Unless something like a religious revolution takes place, I can't see that the Church will ever have any real influence on world affairs.

L.T: Mervyn Porter?

M.P: Naturally, being a priest, I both hope and believe that the Christian Churches will remain a force in the world. At the same time I don't think they should be exclusive. They must find unity among themselves and they must have a closer understanding both of other religions and of people like Jeremy. The new generation of young men who are coming into the priesthood make me hopeful for the future.

NOTES

(1) *The Establishment of the Anglican Church*

The establishment of the Anglican Church dates from the time when Henry VIII broke away from the Church of Rome in 1534. The king declared himself head of the Church in England although after he had defended the papacy against Luther in 1521 the Pope had called him 'Defender of the Faith', a title which the monarch still bears today. The faith which Henry 'defended' was the Catholic faith; he never thought of himself as a Protestant and few real changes were made until after his death.

(2) *The Free (or Nonconformist) Churches*

After the Reformation many Protestants objected that the Church of England had not moved far enough away from the Church of Rome. They broke away from the Church of England and formed their own Churches—the Free or

The Christian Church is re-thinking its role in society—and its attitude to young people.

Nonconformist Churches. As these names suggest, the nonconformists wanted to be free to choose their own form of church organisation and services. They do not have archbishops or bishops and their churches and services are very simple. The main nonconformist groups in England are *Methodist*, *Congregational* and *Baptist*. In 1975 there were 1,150,000 Methodists, 372,000 Congregationalists and 338,000 Baptists. Other groups or sects have moved even further away from the ceremonial approach to religion. Some of these, like the Mormons, the Seventh Day Adventists, the Jehovah's Witnesses and the Christian Scientists (who believe in faith healing of the sick) originated in the United States. The Plymouth Brethren and the Salvation Army are of British origin.

The Salvation Army ('salvation' means 'the saving of souls') was founded in 1865. Its first aim is to preach the story of Jesus Christ to unbelievers and they also do a great deal of social work among the poor and the sick. Their organisation is almost military: they wear a uniform, call themselves officers and their leader has the title of General. Women officers have complete equality with the men. A familiar sight on a Sunday morning in any English town is a group of Salvationists marching through the streets, playing and singing religious music and preaching on street corners. (See picture below.)

The Quakers, or the Society of Friends, was founded in the seventeenth century. They have no ministers and no organised services. They meet on Sundays and speak only when they have something important to say. They frequently worship in silence. They believe strongly in peace and in helping people in trouble. Although they refuse to serve in the armed forces, in time of war they go to the battle front to help the wounded. It is necessary to prove sincerity before being accepted into the Society of Friends. The number of Quakers has increased since 1925. There are now 21,000.

(3) *The Jewish Faith:* There are about 450,000 Jews in Britain—the largest group of Jews in Europe. More than half of them live in London. Jews still tend

to marry Jews, for both racial and religious reasons, though this is happening less and less among the younger generation.

Other religions: Recent immigration has brought increasing numbers of Moslems, Hindus and Sikhs into Britain. The first mosque in the country was built in Woking, Surrey, in 1899, but today there are a number of them in different parts of Britain.

(4) *The Catholic Church in Britain*
The leader of the Catholic Church in Britain is the Cardinal Archbishop of Westminster. The United Kingdom is divided into eight Catholic provinces, four in England, two in Scotland, one each in Wales and Northern Ireland. Each province is controlled by an archbishop and is divided into dioceses which are in the charge of bishops.

(5) *Unity among the Churches*
Today there are signs that the old, narrow intolerance among the Churches is breaking down and many people would like to see greater co-operation and unity. In 1969 the Methodist and Anglican Churches proposed to unite and the proposal failed only because the voting in the Anglican Church assembly was very slightly less than the necessary 75 per cent majority. In spite of this, there are already some churches where Anglican and Methodist ministers share the services and the work in the parish. More recently, the Congregational Church of England and Wales and the Presbyterian Church of England have united and now call themselves the United Reformed Church.

(6) *Episcopal Churches*
There are Churches outside England which are in almost every respect like the Anglican Church; they have the same kind of services and share the same apostolic succession (the passing on through bishops and priests of the powers and mission that was handed on by Christ to his apostles). In Scotland and the United States of America these Churches are called Episcopal Churches (e.g. the Episcopal Church of Scotland).

(7) *The Calvinistic Methodist or Presbyterian Church of Wales*
This is the only Church of purely Welsh origin, drawing its members from a large section of the Welsh-speaking population. It is not an established church (there is no established church in Wales), but it is a member of the British Council of Churches[8] and the World Council of Churches. One of the distinctive features of the Welsh churches is the Sunday school, to which adults as well as children go to study the Bible. In England and Scotland only children attend Sunday school.

(8) *The British Council of Churches*
An official body, presided over by the Archbishop of Canterbury and composed

of representatives of nearly all the Churches in Britain. The Catholic Church sends official observers who take part in the discussions.

(9) *Worker Priests*
A number of Anglican priests now take, with the approval of their bishops, full-time jobs in schools and factories or other places of work.

(10) *Religion in Schools*
Non-denominational religious teaching (i.e. Christian, but not from any one Church) is compulsory in all state schools in England. The school day usually starts with a short service held in the school hall. If a pupil has strong religious or anti-Christian objections he need not attend either the service or the religious lessons. In Scotland, religious teaching and attendance at the morning prayers are not compulsory.

QUESTIONS
(1) Are there any advantages in having an established church like the Churches of England and Scotland?
(2) If you were the Archbishop of Canterbury what would you do to make the Church more up-to-date?
(3) Mervyn Porter feels he is doing more good for a slum family by finding them a home, than by persuading them to come to Church. Do you agree with him?
(4) Should the Church, or churchmen, interfere in political problems?

FURTHER READING

Wilson, Williams and Sugarman	Introduction to Moral Education
Bainton, R.	The Penguin History of Christianity (Vol 2: 1100 to the present day)
Lewis, C. S.	Mere Christianity (Fontana)
Chesterton, G. K.	Orthodoxy (Fontana)
Waugh, E.	Brideshead Revisited (F)
Cary, J.	Except the Lord (M. Joseph) (F)

An open plan primary school—the enviroment reflects the easy-going atmosphere of many modern schools.

A closer look at the project method—with a living audio-visual aid.

9

At School

HOW THE BRITISH TEACH — VARIETY AND
FREEDOM

Elizabeth was visiting a big new secondary
school (see p. 147). As she walked through
the main doors she could hear shouts and
screams coming from a classroom down the
passage.

'Who's being murdered?' she asked the headmaster.

'French aristocrats!' he answered. '4c are acting the French
Revolution in French!'

During the break Elizabeth stood in the playground and watched the
children. The younger ones were playing. The older ones stood in
groups, chatting. In one corner she saw a young teacher surrounded by
a crowd of twelve year olds. They were jumping up and down and
shouting, '*Please*, Miss!'

'What was all that about?' Elizabeth asked the teacher after the
children had gone.

'They want me to take them to the building which is being pulled
down in Bell Street. They want to see the rats there!'

'Good Lord! Why?'

'They're doing a project[1] on the neighbourhood this term. All their
lessons are centred on this project—English, history, geography, and so
on. They even do sums in their maths lessons about the number of cars
made in the local factory. I'm their biology teacher and we're studying
rats at the moment.'

'Will you take them to see the rats?'

'Oh, yes. Rats are a wonderful subject for a lesson!'

Great changes are taking place in British education, encouraged and led by groups of educationists who are always searching for new and progressive ways of teaching, and who believe that children learn best by finding things out for themselves.

'If you interest children they learn so much better,' explained the biology teacher. 'We have a natural history club. You'd be surprised how many children stay behind after school to join the club activities.'

The day before Elizabeth had visited a school in a really tough district where the teachers found it difficult to make the children learn anything. 'Law and Order first' was official school policy. Two boys had been caned[2] that morning for 'running up the stairs'. Elizabeth sensed the 'Them and Us' attitude as soon as she walked through the doors.

Both these schools were state schools, but the difference between them is not so surprising as it may seem. Education in Britain is not as highly centralised as it is in many other countries. The central Department of Education and Science in London guides, advises and inspects, (which means it sends its inspectors round to schools to see that they are efficient), but the planning and organisation of education in England and Wales is in the hands of the 82 Local Education Authorities (L.E.A.s for short).

The L.E.A.s are controlled by the Education Committees of the county and metropolitan district councils (see p. 87 Note 10). Most of the money comes from the general grant provided by the Treasury (see p. 83). But the government interferes as little as possible with the activities of the L.E.A.s and of the schools. In the same way, the L.E.A.s interfere as little as possible with headmasters and headmistresses, who, in their turn allow a great deal of freedom to the staff. Teachers choose their own books and are free to experiment in many different ways.

But Charles Blakeney is not entirely happy about the state of British education.

'We don't encourage enough students to go in for technology. We desperately need more trained engineers.'

STATE (NON FEE-PAYING) SCHOOLS

Grammar schools provide an academic education and are intended for those who may wish to go on to higher education or professional training. Secondary modern schools teach some academic subjects, but at a lower level and are essentially for children who are unlikely to go on

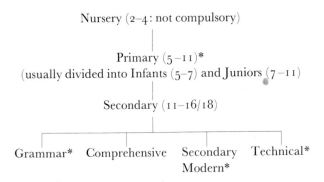

to higher education. The few technical schools specialise in technical subjects. Comprehensive schools—the word means 'all-inclusive'—are grammar, secondary modern and technical schools rolled into one.

All state schools are controlled by L.E.A.s. About half the money comes from the Treasury, the rest from rates. Each school has a board of governors or managers, a group of well-known local citizens who give their services to the school free. The governors take part in the appointment of the headmaster, and also help him to appoint the staff.

Before 1976 there was another type of secondary school—the direct grant school. There were 173 of them. These schools were not controlled by the L.E.A.s. They got money direct from the Treasury, provided they offered 25 per cent of their places to pupils from L.E.A. primary schools. The rest of their money came from fee-paying pupils. Then the Labour government refused them any more Treasury grants. They were given the choice of going comprehensive under L.E.A.s or becoming independent. Most of them went independent. If the Conservatives win the next election, they will restore grants to direct grant schools, and might try to bring back as many grammar schools as possible.

Church schools (mostly Anglican and Roman Catholic) also receive aid from the L.E.A.s and are not fee-paying.

Education is free and compulsory from the ages of five to sixteen.

GARETH AND JIM GO TO STATE SCHOOLS

Gareth and Jim Williams went to the same primary school. Then, at the age of eleven they each went, without taking any exams, to the local comprehensive. Gareth was put in the top 'stream'. Jim was put in one

* Some L.E.A.s have bridged the division between primary and secondary education with a three-tier system (one on top of the other) of first schools (5–9), middle schools (8/9–12/13) and secondary or high schools (12/13–16/18). In 1976 comprehensive education was made compulsory for all L.E.A. schools, though there are still a few grammar and secondary schools left.

of the bottom streams. He was one of the 80% who would have gone in the old days to a secondary modern. Gareth immediately went to the top of his class. Jim was soon at the bottom of his, and he stayed there until he left school at sixteen. 'Not without ability, but difficult and lazy,' said his school reports.

'He's a bright lad, really,' said Jim's probation officer, 'and he's good with his hands. He'd have made a good mechanic.'

But Jim left school with no qualifications whatsoever.

'The trouble with Jim's comprehensive,' said the probation officer, 'is that it's like a grammar school and a bad secondary modern rolled into one. The staff aren't interested in the kids down at the bottom. Now if he'd gone to the new comprehensive at Cannon Corner....'

Ever since the first comprehensive school was opened (under a Labour government) in 1945, there have been bitter arguments for and against this 'revolution'. In 1965 'comprehensive education for all' became official Labour policy, and all the L.E.A.s were officially requested to produce plans to 'go comprehensive'. Very few refused, although the Conservative Party immediately replied with their battle-cry 'Save the grammar schools!'

When the Conservatives won the 1970 election, they at once told the L.E.A.s that they could forget the Labour government's 'request'. But by then nearly all the L.E.A.s, whether Conservative or Labour controlled, had gone so far along the comprehensive road that they could not draw back.

COMPREHENSIVE SCHOOLS

Charles Blakeney is a governor of a well-known boys' grammar school. He and Elizabeth Townsend met one day at a party and talked about comprehensive and grammar schools.

CHARLES: It'll be a sad day if all grammar schools go comprehensive, but I don't think it'll happen.

ELIZABETH: You're against comprehensives, Mr Blakeney? Why?

CHARLES: They're too big. Two thousand children under one roof? That's an unmanageable number. Besides, I don't believe in putting gifted and less gifted children together. It's unfair to both, particularly to the top 10 per cent. Lord knows, our bright children deserve the best training they can get these days. We need them!

ELIZABETH: I think you've got the wrong idea about comprehensives. In

Two extremes—a new London comprehensive school, which all the children in the area can attend, and Harrow, one of the most exclusive of boys' public schools.

147

districts which have gone *completely* comprehensive, exam results are better than ever before. More children are staying on at school till seventeen or eighteen, and more are getting to university. Eleven plus[4] selection is very unfair to too many children, especially to late-developers.

CHARLES: I thought that most L.E.A.s had done away with the eleven plus.

ELIZABETH: They have. That's one reason why our primary schools are so good. They can forget about exams now and think more about education. But we must get rid of the eleven plus altogether. A comprehensive system is no good unless it's complete.

CHARLES: It's an unjust world, Mrs Townsend, but we can't afford to be unjust to our clever children.

ELIZABETH: Don't think me rude, Mr Blakeney, but if your parents hadn't been able to afford to send you to a private school perhaps *you* would have failed the eleven plus! And that would have been a waste, wouldn't it! But it's what the eleven plus does to people that worries me most. Children who've been friends at primary school often stop seeing each other when they're separated into secondary modern and grammar schools. There's a kind of shame in failing the eleven plus which even rubs off onto parents.

CHARLES: You get the same sort of divisions inside comprehensives, I've heard. The academic and non-academic children just don't mix.

ELIZABETH: Where do you draw the line between academic and non-academic? Lots of children with no academic background become interested in serious work just by being with studious children. That's one of the great advantages of comprehensives. Besides, they do mix quite a lot—on the sports field, in the school choir, in school clubs. They have lunch together, and so on.

CHARLES: You're not suggesting that all comprehensives are good, surely? Some L.E.A.s have just put their grammar and secondary modern schools together and *called* them comprehensives—even though the two parts are at opposite ends of the town! Ask the teachers of the top classes in these schools what they think of the system. You won't find them very enthusiastic!

ELIZABETH: That's not an argument against the system. It just underlines the need for more buildings.

CHARLES: There's a very large comprehensive close to the grammar school of which I'm a governor. The comprehensive doesn't get nearly such good exam results as the grammar school. Why do you think this happens, Mrs Townsend?

ELIZABETH: Because the grammar school gets the academic 'cream' of the neighbourhood. Any school can get good exam results with *clever* children.

CHARLES: But why do parents send their children to grammar schools if they have the choice?

ELIZABETH: Partly for snobbish reasons, and partly because they often don't realise how good the comprehensives are. I'm quite sure that a clever boy from the comprehensive you've mentioned would get to a university just as easily as a clever boy from your grammar school.

BOYS AND GIRLS TOGETHER

Many people in Britain today are talking about the advantages and disadvantages of co-education. More and more schools are going co-educational.

'What do you feel about boys and girls together in the same school, Mr Blakeney?' asked Elizabeth.

'Well, personally I wouldn't have liked to have a pretty girl sitting beside me in the classroom! I'd have found it—well, disturbing.'

Elizabeth laughed.

'Isn't this even worse in single-sex schools? The headmaster of a big boys' grammar school once told me he couldn't get any work out of his boys after three o'clock. They all had their eyes on the clock, because they had dates with girls from the girls' school down the road! Boys and girls in co-educational schools get so used to one another that they aren't disturbed. After all, it isn't natural to keep the sexes apart.'

PRIVATE OR INDEPENDENT (FEE-PAYING) SCHOOLS

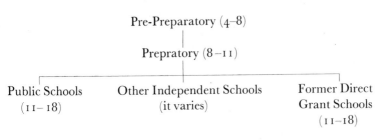

Pre-Preparatory (4–8)
|
Prepratory (8–11)

Public Schools (11–18) | Other Independent Schools (it varies) | Former Direct Grant Schools (11–18)

The public schools are the most famous of the private schools. The oldest of the public schools (Eton College was founded in 1440) were founded to give free education to clever boys whose parents could not afford to educate them privately. They were under 'public' management or control. Today, these schools, and similar ones founded within the past 120 years, are the most expensive of the independent schools in Britain. They are mostly boarding schools, where the pupils live as well as study, though many of them also take some day-pupils. Most of them have a few places for pupils whose fees are paid by a local authority, but normally entrance is by examination and state schools do not prepare children for this. So parents who wish to send their children to a public school often send them first to a preparatory (prep) school. Preparatory schools are small, private primary schools which *prepare* children for the public school examination.

Public schools have produced many of Britain's most famous and distinguished men and women and many parents are still ready to make great sacrifices in order to send their children there. Other people see them as a continuation of privilege and a stronghold of Britain's upper and wealthy classes. Recently, therefore, there has been a great deal of argument about the future of all private schools.

PUBLIC SCHOOLS

If Anne and Charles have a son, Anne wants him to go to a state school. Charles, however, wants him to go to Eton—he went to Eton himself. So did Sir Eric and generations of Blakeney boys before him. Between the ages of fourteen and eighteen, Charles spent two-thirds of each year as a boarder inside its ancient walls.

'It made a man of him!' Sir Eric claims.

Sir Eric is sure that the discipline and masculinity of public school life, with its emphasis on games, builds character and encourages team spirit. He is extremely proud that Charles played cricket for Eton.

'You know the old saying,' he said. ' "The Battle of Waterloo was won on the playing fields of Eton!" You may laugh, Anne, but public schools teach leadership.'

'You're out-of-date, Father,' said Charles. 'A lot of today's leaders didn't go to a public school.'

'Well!' said Anne, when they were alone. 'You argued like that against your father, and yet you want our son to go to Eton! Why?'

'For purely practical reasons. The classes are smaller than those of the average grammar or comprehensive school. There are more out-of-school activities—music, art, discussion groups and so on—and more time to give to them. Eton's a very progressive school, in fact. Father doesn't realise it, but games are no longer compulsory! Besides, there are some brilliant masters. So there should be! The top twenty public schools can afford to pay higher salaries than the state.'

'What about the public schools that don't belong to the top twenty? Take the one we visited last Sunday. The buildings were dark and dirty. The teachers were dull and ordinary, and the only thing the headmaster could talk about was the cricket matches his team had won! Be honest! Some parents still send their sons to public schools because they think it'll get them better jobs. The public school tradition isn't dead. There's still the snob value.'

'Not so much these days. When I make appointments I don't bother about what school a person went to.'

'It's a pity you don't appoint our politicians, then!—over 60 per cent of Conservative M.P.s are from public schools, and about fifty M.P.s come from Eton alone!'

'Most of them are no better or no worse than the Labour M.P.s who went to grammar or secondary modern schools,' said Charles.

SCHOOL EXAMINATIONS

	Age at which usually taken
General Certificate of Education at Ordinary Level (G.C.E. 'O' level)	15/16
Certificate of Secondary Education (C.S.E.)	15/16
General Certificate of Education at Advanced Level (G.C.E. 'A' level)	17/18
Oxford and Cambridge Scholarship Examinations	18/19

G.C.E. 'O' and 'A' level examinations are set and marked by various examining boards appointed by universities or groups of universities. Schools can choose which board they like. Both 'O' and 'A' levels can be taken in almost any subject. The average grammar and public school candidate takes six or seven 'O' levels, the most common subjects being English, history, geography, French, German, mathematics, chemistry, physics and biology. Latin is much less common than it used to be, since it is no longer a compulsory qualification for arts courses in universities.

Good 'O' level passes qualify boys and girls for good office jobs and for entry to courses for certain specialist jobs. Good 'A' level passes are essential for entrance into a university and the number of subjects taken at 'A' level varies between one and four. A combination of arts and science subjects is possible, but not usual. Students apply for a place at university through the Universities Central Council on Admissions and can have a choice of up to five universities, which they state in order of preference. Whether they can go to their first choice depends on how good their 'A' level results are and the number of places that are being offered.

The C.S.E. examination is like 'O' level, but less academic in its approach; in other words, it is usually more suited to modern methods of teaching which include a great deal of project work. It is marked by teachers and has nothing to do with the universities.

CLASSES

Classes in British secondary schools are usually (though not always) called 'forms'; they are never called 'grades', which is an American term. Forms are numbered from one to six, beginning with the first form and ending with the sixth form. The G.C.E. 'O' levels are usually taken at the end of the year in the fifth form, but other subjects may be taken in the sixth form. 'A' levels are usually taken at the end of the second year in the sixth form[5].

GARETH AND CHRISTINE AND THEIR EXAMINATIONS

Gareth, like many of his teachers, is very critical of both 'O' and 'A' level examinations.

'They're not in step with modern ways of teaching,' he told Christine. 'From the fourth form onwards you learn in order to pass exams, which often have nothing to do with education. You're just filled full of lots of facts. Take English. We had a wonderful teacher who loved exploring all the latest and strangest modern authors. But for 'O' level we had to study books set by the examining boards, most of which none of us liked.'

'I know,' said Christine. 'I had a wonderful French teacher who talked French to us all the time. We loved it and learned to speak fluently. But most of us failed 'O' level French because he didn't teach us how to translate.'

Gareth is also angry that he had to specialise so young.

'Nothing but science in the sixth form!' he said. 'I know I could have taken English or history instead of maths, but I didn't dare to, because I want to be a scientist. There's not enough time given to general studies in the sixth form, and anyway, boys don't take them seriously because there's no exam in them.'

Dissatisfaction with the G.C.E. is so great, especially among progressive teachers, that by the time the Macdonald twins reach the sixth form, there will probably be an entirely new examination system.

The Schools Council, which is the body responsible for advising on new teaching methods and examinations, has recommended many improvements and some of these have already been introduced.

NOTES

(1) *Project Work*
The project method is now a basic part of English infant and junior education and also of many secondary schools. Projects may be anything from organising an entertainment to producing a magazine. They are given to single pupils or to groups, and their purpose is to encourage the students to work things out for themselves. (Many older boys and girls today prefer to be called students.)

(2) *Caning* (beating with a stick)
This form of punishment is still used in some schools, though many people think that it is wrong. In 1971 the Inner London Education Authority forbade caning in all primary schools. Many headmasters have either given up the practice or use it very rarely. In a few public schools, caning is still carried out by prefects, older boys who have positions of authority.

(3) *The Growth of Comprehensives*

1964	1973	1974	1975
195	1,835	2,273	2,596

In 1975 there were already more comprehensives than grammar and secondary moderns combined. In 1964 there were 1,298 grammar schools. In 1975 there were 566.

(4) *The eleven plus examination*
Until recently, this was a selective examination taken at the age of ten or eleven, to decide who should go to grammar schools. Educationalists regarded it as a

very unfair test for such young children. The number who passed varied from 10% to 45%, depending on the county.

(5) *Sixth Form Colleges*
These are separate colleges for students between the ages of sixteen and eighteen. Such colleges were first discussed in the 1960s, when it became clear that the secondary schools would not have room for all students wishing to stay on at school after the age of sixteen. Not all L.E.A.s have introduced sixth form colleges (there are about 60 of them). But colleges of further education offer 'A' level courses as well as many different vocational courses—secretarial, building etc. (See p. 164.)

(6) *Numbers at school*
Number of full-time pupils in January, 1973—9,190,030

    a) Primary   5,148,965
         Secondary   3,362,554
    b) L.E.A. schools   8,648,276
         Former Direct Grant schools   130,090
         Independent schools   411,664
pupil/teacher ratio (England and Wales) — 20·2:1

(7) *The School Year*
The school year is divided into three terms.
      Autumn term: early September to mid-December
      Spring term: early January to the end of March/beginning of April
      Summer term: end of April to early/mid-July.
School hours are usually from 9.00 a.m. until 3.30 or 4.00 p.m.

(8) *Teachers' Qualifications*
Every new teacher in a state school must have taken a teacher-training course. Most teachers qualify by completing a three-year training course at a college of education and receiving a teaching certificate. Many colleges now provide students with a four-year course leading to a B.Ed. degree. University students who wish to teach can spend an extra year, after taking their degrees, at the department of education in a university. All teacher-training courses include practical experience in the classroom.

(9) *Scottish Education*
The Scottish Education Department is the government body responsible for education in Scotland (it is the Scottish equivalent of the Department of Education and Science, which is the central authority for education in England and Wales). Comprehensive education provided the framework for the Scottish system before the English began to think about it on a national scale. Another important difference in Scottish education is that the age for moving from the primary to secondary schools is twelve, not eleven as in England. Few Scottish children go to public schools.

QUESTIONS

(1) The advantages of project work are made fairly clear in this chapter. What are the disadvantages?

↘(2) Do you learn best by finding things out for yourself?

(3) Should teachers have the right to beat children?

(4) Can you understand why the Labour Party has put an end to direct grant schools? Do you agree with private education?

(5) There are many arguments in this chapter for and against selection at eleven. Can you add more?

FURTHER READING

Burgess, T.	A Guide to English Schools
Lester Smith, W. O.	Education
Rubinstein and Stoneman, ed.	Education for Democracy
Blishen, E. ed.	The School that I'd Like
Partridge, J.	Life in a Secondary Modern School
Spark, M.	The Prime of Miss Jean Brodie (F)

Graduation. In most
universities the
traditional academic
gowns are worn only on
special occasions like
this.

10

Universities and Colleges

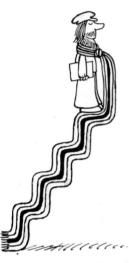

UNIVERSITIES AND COLLEGES

British universities can be divided roughly into three main groups.

The old universities: Oxford and Cambridge are the oldest universities. Scholars were studying there in the early thirteenth century. Since that time they have continued to grow, the most recent additions being in 1965 and 1966. Until the nineteenth century, Oxford and Cambridge were the only two universities in England, and there was no place for girls (see Note 2).

In the fourteenth and fifteenth centuries, four universities were founded in Scotland: St. Andrews (1411), Glasgow (1450), Aberdeen (1494) and Edinburgh (1583).

The redbrick universities: These include all the provincial universities of the period 1850–1930, as well as London University. The term 'redbrick' is not used much today, but it is a useful way of describing this group of universities, many of which were built in the favourite building material of the time—red brick.

The new universities: These are all the universities founded since the second world war. Because of their more modern approach to university courses, some students choose the new universities in preference to other universities. But Oxford and Cambridge are still the main attraction.

Altogether, there are now forty-six universities in the United Kingdom: thirty-five in England, eight in Scotland, two in Northern Ireland and one, a federation of seven colleges, in Wales.

'My chemistry teacher wants me to go to Cambridge,' Gareth said to Christine. 'But I'm not sure I wouldn't prefer a new university. Of course, Mum wants me to go to London University—so that I can live at home!'

'Why don't you go and talk to the Robinsons?' said Christine. 'They should be able to help you make up your mind. They've been picked to take part in a BBC discussion on universities next week.'

The Robinsons live next door to Christine, Henry Robinson is twenty-two and is in his last year at Cambridge. Liz Robinson is twenty and is at a redbrick university in a northern industrial city. Patricia, who is nineteen, has just started at one of the new universities.

Patricia's university, like several of the other new universities, is on the edge of an ancient cathedral city, about two miles from the centre. It is planned on the American 'campus' system, that is to say, students live in halls of residence grouped around the main university buildings.

'I like it because we're a real community,' said Patricia. 'We've got comfortable common rooms and bars. We arrange dances and parties. We've got clubs, theatre groups, choirs and so on. And we've got an orchestra. I play the drums in it.'

'We've got bars and common rooms and clubs too,' said Liz. 'But I'd hate to live in the sort of closed community you live in, Pat.'

Liz and two other girls rent a house in the middle of the city, about ten minutes' walk from the university. The house is falling to pieces. It is damp, and there is no proper heating. The district is poor and could almost be classed as a slum.

'I couldn't work in a place like yours,' said Henry.

'Nor could I!' said Patricia.

'You're a couple of snobs!' said Liz. 'We live among real people, who treat *us* as real people. We've got an electrician living next door who's always coming in and mending our cooker and electric fires. We could try to get into one of the halls of residence, but we prefer to be independent. It's nice to *belong* to the city and to do things outside the university. Besides, from the way you talk sometimes, anyone would think that university students were the only students. In our city there are nearly 15,000 full-time students, and only about 5,000 of them are at university. The rest of them are at different kinds of colleges—'.

'Doing what?' asked Henry.

'Learning to be tradesmen, technicians, craftsmen, artists, teachers and so on. The north's not all smoke and smells you know!'

'What sort of things do you do outside the university, Pat?' asked Gareth.

'Well, there's a group of us who go and help in a home for handicapped children. And I sing in the city Bach choir. We get on well with the local people—not like Henry and the people in Cambridge!'

'Oh, most of us get on very well with the local people,' said Henry. 'Cambridge isn't a big place.'

'So you're not sorry you chose Cambridge?' Gareth asked.

'No, I'm reading chemistry and Cambridge is one of the best universities for any science subject. Besides, Cambridge, like Oxford, has got a special atmosphere. It has a great effect on you, this atmosphere, especially if you live in one of the old colleges.'

All 'Oxbridge' (Oxford and Cambridge) students belong to a college[2], and the college is the centre of their university life.

'It's like living in a community within a community,' said Henry.

There is great rivalry between colleges, both academically and on the sports field. As Henry explained to Gareth:

'Some colleges boast that they produce the best scholars, but at my college we produce the best rugger players!'

STUDY AND DEGREES[3]

Only about 10 per cent of British students leave university without getting a degree[4]. Henry is not worried about failing, but he is very anxious to get a *good* degree. He is aiming for a first class honours degree in chemistry, because he wants a scientific post in industry.

In Henry's case everything will depend on how well he does in his 'finals' at the end of his third and last year. He finds the uncertainty a great strain. Patricia, on the other hand, will not have so great a strain, for although she too will have to take a final exam, she will also get marks for the work she does during her three years at university. These marks will count towards her degree, and will play an important part in deciding whether she gets first, second or third class honours. Many universities have changed and modernised their examination systems.

Patricia chose her university because of its progressive ideas on education and its broader and more varied courses. Many of the new universities are experimenting with new subjects.

'I'm doing comparative literature,' she said. 'At the moment I'm comparing English, French and Russian novels. We write papers on our work, and then about ten of us meet with our professor and read them and discuss them.'

This 'seminar' system is common in the new universities.

'It works, because we get on well with the professors and lecturers,' said Patricia. 'Some of them aren't much older than us and they don't mind at all if we disagree with them.'

'You're lucky!' said Liz. 'We have classes, but we hardly ever ask questions or discuss anything. It's partly our fault. We're a dull lot, but so are the profs. They don't seem to be able to do anything but lecture. Besides, the course itself is so out-of-date. It hasn't changed in the last twenty years. I think students ought to have a say in planning and changing their programmes of study.'

'It wouldn't work,' said Henry. 'There'd be too many different opinions.'

Henry, like Liz, is critical of his professors and lecturers, some of whom are more interested in their own research than in helping him in his studies. However, he attends lectures given by some of the most brilliant scholars in the country.

Henry goes to classes as well as to lectures, but the most important person in his academic life is his tutor who, in Cambridge, is called a supervisor. Henry enjoys his weekly tutorials. His supervisor is an approachable man and is always ready to talk to him about anything connected with his work.

'Haven't other universities now introduced some form of tutorial supervision?' asked Gareth.

'Yes,' said Henry. 'In fact, to be honest, there are universities which offer better courses and give better teaching in some subjects than either Oxford or Cambridge. I think that an Oxbridge degree still counts more with some employers than a degree from other universities, but most of them are more concerned with the *kind* of degree than where it comes from.'

Both Henry and Patricia think that personal supervision and friendly relations with the teaching staff are especially good at British universities. They have no complaints, either, about the lecturer-student ratio[6].

'I'm not so sure,' said Liz, 'but at least we're not overcrowded. I've

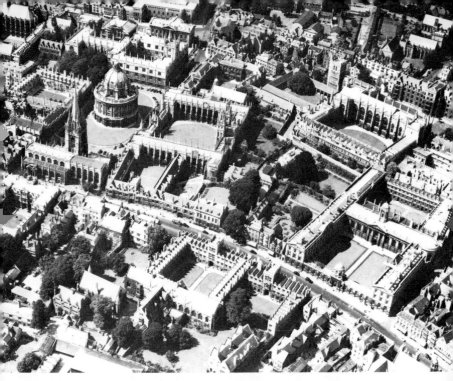

Oxford university is inseparable from the city, whereas the University of East Anglia has its own spacious and landscaped campus.

heard that in some foreign universities lecture halls are packed so full that students have nowhere to sit.'

In 1970 there were twice as many students as in 1960, but universities are no longer expanding so rapidly. However, accommodation is still a problem. Most universities have hostels or rooms, but not enough for everyone. So all the rest have to find somewhere to live in the neighbouring town. Very few students choose universities near their home.

WHO PAYS?

Mr Robinson, who is a manager in a small department store, cannot afford to pay for his children's education at university. Since they were all able to get the necessary 'A' levels at school, each of them receives a grant from the local council. This covers all their fees and living expenses during term time.

If Charles Blakeney had a son of university age, however, he would have to pay both fees and living expenses. The size of the L.E.A. grant depends on the size of the parents' income.

UNIVERSITIES AND THE STATE—STUDENT UNREST

The following is an extract from a discussion on television about British universities. Taking part are Leonard Townsend (chairman), a Vice-Chancellor (the head of a university), Jeremy Martin, Liz and Patricia Robinson.

LEONARD TOWNSEND: Like every other traditional institution, the universities have had their fair share of criticisms recently, haven't they, Vice-Chancellor? Most of the criticisms have come from the students themselves, often supported by some of the younger lecturers. But we'll come back to that in a minute. I'd like to start our discussion by asking you a different kind of question. Which feature of our university system would you defend above all others?

VICE-CHANCELLOR: The freedom and independence of the universities. The state has no say in the way they are run, although it provides them with most of the money they need. Each university is like an independent country, with its own government and its own special character.

L.T: Does this explain why some universities have student troubles and some have none?

V.C: Certainly, because some universities have more student participation than others, and participation rather than politics is what most student troubles are about.

L.T: Jeremy, when you were president of your students' union, you declared on many occasions that there was no true student participation in *any* university.

JEREMY: There isn't. Even at universities where students do send representatives to administration meetings, they have no real power. They feel they are there only as observers.

LIZ: I agree with Jeremy. We have the right to vote at eighteen. We're supposed to be full and equal citizens, but at university we're often treated like school children.

L.T: Can you explain, Liz, why at Jeremy's university there has been so much unrest, while at yours there has been practically none?

LIZ: Because at my university the majority of students are studying medicine or agriculture. They haven't time to protest. They're too busy thinking about their future jobs! Jeremy's university has very strong political and social science faculties, and, after all, these subjects do encourage people to question and criticise institutions.

JEREMY: That's nonsense—at least, it's nonsense if you're implying that only students of political and social sciences want more say in what's going on. What about the trouble they had at some of the art colleges? Their students weren't interested in politics, but they wanted proper conditions to work in and more relevant courses.

L.T: Jeremy was at a new university. You, Patricia, are also at a new university. Yet you have no trouble. Why?

PATRICIA: We haven't really found anything to rebel against—yet! We get on very well with the staff, particularly the younger lecturers and professors. They invite us to parties, and stop and talk to us out of class and so on. And our student representatives do seem to have some influence, even on the more elderly administrators. We have very few old-fashioned rules. For example, men and women students can visit each other's rooms and have parties as late as they like.

V.C: This isn't so unusual, you know. Many Vice-Chancellors and their councils are sensible and human enough to smell trouble before it comes. So they bring in reforms and avoid it.

163

JEREMY: Yes, but you must admit, Vice-Chancellor, that over and over again sensible reforms have only been brought in after strong protests or sit-ins by students.

OTHER COLLEGES FOR FURTHER EDUCATION

Polytechnics: The polytechnics could be called the 'comprehensives' of further education. They are study centres that offer many different full-time or part-time courses for students of all ages (usually over eighteen). Courses lead to diplomas, or to degrees awarded by the Council for National Academic Awards (C.N.A.A.), a body which was set up in 1964 to award degrees to students taking approved courses in non-university institutions.

Other kinds of colleges: There are various specialist colleges such as the National Colleges for advanced technical studies for industry, Agricultural Colleges, Colleges of Art or Music, and so on. There are also a large number of local colleges of further education, technical colleges and colleges of commerce which provide a variety of courses for full or part-time students.

Adult education: Courses for adults may be vocational or recreational, that is, they may be related to a person's job or taken purely for interest and pleasure. Such courses are provided mainly by local authorities, the Workers Educational Association, and by the extramural (i.e. for activities outside the institution) departments of universities and colleges. Examples of popular recreational classes are pottery, where people learn to make pots and vases; woodwork; car maintenance; cookery, etc. At the same time, university lecturers may give up some of their free time every week to talk to town and village clubs about anything from archaeology to the sociological effects of the industrial revolution.

Altogether, there are several million full-time and part-time students at polytechnics, L.E.A. colleges and evening institutes—their ages ranging between sixteen and eighty!

Part-time education: Every young worker who joins the Blakeney firm spends one day a week—with pay—at a technical college or college of further education. Some take specialist courses in their particular skill, and work for a diploma. Others just 'go back to school', and study general subjects like English, maths and history. It was Charles who persuaded his father to take this step.

'You get better work out of an educated workman,' he said. 'Besides, firms which offer further education of this sort attract a better kind of workman. I've actually got a promising young mechanic studying for an engineering degree at a polytechnic.'

There is no law which forces employers to send their young workers to these colleges, but every employer has to pay a 'Further Education Tax' whether he takes advantage of the system or not. Herbert Perkins considers the tax to be unfair.

'What are you grumbling about, Herbert?' said Charles. 'If you sent your workers to classes you'd get your money back in the form of a generous training grant. That's the whole idea of the tax. It's meant to encourage old reactionaries like you to be progressive!'

'It's a waste of time and public money,' replied Herbert. 'Do you think learning about "1066 and all that" helps my shop girls to sell more biscuits and bacon? If they want to better themselves they should go to evening classes in their spare time—as I did.'

THE OPEN UNIVERSITY

In 1963 the leader of the Labour Party made a speech explaining plans for a 'university of the air'—an educational system which would make use of television, radio and correspondence courses. Many people laughed at the idea, but it became part of the Labour Party's programme, to give educational opportunity to those people who, for one reason or another, had not had a chance to receive further education. By 1969 plans were well advanced and by August 1970 the Open University, as it was now called, had received 40,000 applications. Only 25,000 could be accepted for the four 'foundation' (introductory) courses offered: social sciences, arts, science and mathematics. Unsuccessful candidates were told to apply again the following year, when a foundation course in technology would also be offered.

The first teaching programmes appeared on the air and screen in January 1971, with clerks, farm workers, housewives, teachers, policemen and many others as students. Correspondence units had been carefully prepared and science students were given apparatus for a 'mini' home laboratory. Study centres have been set up all over the country so that students can attend once a week, and once a year they spend a week at one of the university's summer schools.

It is too early yet to say how successful this new university will be. Its critics complain of the cost, but the Open University is probably the cheapest and most far-reaching method yet found of spreading further education.

NOTES

(1) *The 'Technological' Universities*
During the 1960s the best of the many technical colleges (which were supported by the local authorities) were given the status of universities. Although their main studies are still in the scientific and technological subjects, they have introduced other subjects such as languages and social sciences. Many of these former 'techs' were in large cities where there was already a university, so there are now some towns and cities in Britain which have two universities.

The rapidly expanding field of adult education—people have an opportunity to find out what and how their children learn, or to develop an interest of their own.

(2) *The College System*

The college system at Oxford and Cambridge is unlike that of any other university, whether in Britain or America. In order to enter the university, a student must first apply to a college and become a member of the university through the college. The colleges are not connected with any particular study and are governed by twenty to thirty 'Fellows'. Each Fellow of a college is a 'tutor' (a teacher, often called a don). He teaches his own subject to those students in his college who are studying it, and is responsible for their progress.

The university is like a federation of colleges. The university arranges the courses, the lectures, and the examinations, and awards the degrees. Most dons give one or two lectures a week which students from any college may attend. No lectures are compulsory and tutors usually advise their students which lectures they should go to.

Each college has its own completely separate living quarters, its own dining hall and its own chapel. Cambridge has three women's colleges, Oxford five. Today some of the men's colleges are going co-educational.

The University of London could also be called a kind of federation of colleges, but the system is entirely different. The largest of the London colleges are like universities in themselves, having many different faculties and departments. Others specialise in certain subjects, for example the London School of Economics and Political Science or the Imperial College of Science and Technology. All arrange their own lectures and classes, but the university organises the examinations and awards degrees.

(3) *Degrees*

A degree course normally takes three or four years. There are two kinds of degrees—honours and pass (or general). An honours degree is taken in one or two related subjects (e.g. two foreign languages) and is graded as first, second or third class. The pass degree includes several subjects, studied in less depth than is required for an honours degree. A student who gets a first degree becomes a Bachelor of Arts or Science (B.A. and B.Sc.). An M.A. or M.Sc. (Master of Arts/Science) degree may be obtained by attending a postgraduate course or by doing some original work and writing a paper, or thesis. A Ph.D (Doctor of Philosophy) and other higher degrees are awarded for research work. Two rather curious facts should be mentioned:

    i) an Oxford or Cambridge B.A. can buy his M.A. without doing any further work at all, seven years after his admission to the university.

    ii) in Scotland, an M.A. is the equivalent of the English B.A.

(4) *Degrees* (1971–2)
    a) university honours degrees: 41,444
    b) university general degrees: 10,338

(5) *Admission to universities* (October 1974)
    number applying: 125,780
    number accepted: 69,005

A student sit-in at the Rutherford College of Technology.

(6) *Number of students*
    a) at universities (full-time) — undergraduates   199,907
                                      — postgraduates   46,906
    b) at other institutions of higher education (full-time)
       in colleges of education   127,600
    c) doing advanced courses, including sandwich
       courses (i.e. theory and practical experience
       with firms)   107,900
       Staff/student ratio at universities: 1:8

(7) *Number of students per 100,000 of population* (1966)
    UK   646
    Italy   659
    Germany   708
    France   1,076
    Sweden   1,079
    USA   3,245

(8) *University terms*
October–December; January–March; April–June.
Total: six to eight months of the year.

(9) *Type of school attended by students accepted at universities* (1973–4)

L.E.A. schools	53 per cent
Direct Grant schools (now either comprehensive or independent)	13·5 per cent
Independent schools	15·1 per cent
Institutions of further education	13·2 per cent
Other schools and institutions	5·2 per cent

(10) *Proportion of national income spent on education*

Switzerland	4·3 per cent
W. Germany	4·5 per cent
Italy	4·8 per cent
Yugoslavia	5·5 per cent
UK	5·9 per cent
USA	6·7 per cent
Sweden	7·9 per cent

QUESTIONS

(1) Would you tolerate the conditions Liz Robinson lives in, in order to go to a university?

(2) Would you prefer to take a final exam, or be given marks throughout the course?

(3) Henry and Liz disagree about students planning their own courses. Can you add further reasons to those they give?

(4) What are the advantages of the system of studying while working, as practised in Charles' factory? Could this form of study take the place of study in the closed community of the university?

FURTHER READING

Peters, A. J.	British Further Education (Pergamon)
Brosan et al.	Patterns and Policies in Higher Education
Daiches, ed.	The Idea of a New University (Deutsch)
Blackburn and Cockburn, ed.	Student Power
Amis, K.	Lucky Jim (F)
Beerbohm, M.	Zuleika Dobson (F)
Snow, C. P.	The Masters (F)

Fleet Street — the centre of the newspaper industry.

11

The Press, Television and Radio

It has been claimed that the British read more newspapers than any other people in the western world. More than thirty million copies of newspapers are printed in the country every day.

THE NATIONAL PRESS

National newspapers are sold throughout the United Kingdom. They all have their head offices in London and are usually classed as either 'quality' or 'popular' papers. The quality papers (dailies: *The Times, Guardian, Daily Telegraph*; Sunday papers: *Sunday Times, Observer, Sunday Telegraph*) aim to inform their readers as widely as possible about national and international news. The popular papers try to attract more general readers, with pictures and sensational stories. The *News of the World* has the largest circulation of any newspaper in the western world.

The chart on page 174 gives the circulation figures for 1974. Only one national newspaper, *The Morning Star*, is the *official* mouthpiece of a political party, but many of the other papers support a political party *unofficially*. The quality papers could be called 'independent', except for the Daily Telegraph and Sunday Telegraph, which support the Conservatives. The Daily Mail and Daily Express are usually Conservative in sympathy. The Daily Mirror and the Sun support Labour.

THE PROVINCIAL PRESS (published outside London)

The three most famous provincial daily newspapers are *The Scotsman*

(Edinburgh), *Glasgow Herald* and *Yorkshire Post*, which present national as well as local news. *The Scotsman* and *Glasgow Herald* could be considered 'national' papers for Scotland and all three have a high standard of reporting. A few others, like the *Western Mail* (Cardiff) and *Birmingham Post*, have a good standard but are less well known. Apart from these, there are many other daily, evening and weekly papers published in cities and smaller towns. They present local news and are supported by local advertisements, but the standard of writing is not always very high.

EVENING NEWSPAPERS

Many big cities have evening papers which give the latest news. London has two, *The Evening Standard* and *The Evening News*, which have circulations of 520,000 and 818,000 respectively.

HEADLINES AND POSTERS

There was a pile of evening newspapers on the pavement outside the underground station. 'Read all about it!' shouted the man selling them. On either side of him, leaning against the wall, were two large posters. One said, 'Latest Racing Results', the other, 'Famous Actress Dies in Bath'.

Leonard Townsend, who was on his way home, bought both *The Standard* and *The News*. 'Which actress?' he wondered. 'She could be someone I've interviewed.'

There was nothing about the actress on the front page. ELECTION SHOCKS IN USA was the headline on one. POLICE SEARCH FOREST FOR MURDERER was the headline on the other. He turned the pages. At last he found it. 'Milly Minter, well-known comic actress of the 1920s, died peacefully in her bath this morning. She was eighty-three.' That was all. There was nothing about Milly in the other paper. This didn't surprise Leonard because he had never heard of her.

PERIODICALS (published weekly, monthly or quarterly)

There are nearly 5,000 periodicals published in the United Kingdom. Of these, women's magazines have the largest circulations: *Woman*, (1,700,000) and *Woman's Own*, (1,660,000).

There are magazines and periodicals for almost every trade,

profession, sport, hobby or interest. The most important periodicals for the more serious readers are: *The Economist*, which comments on events of international, political or economic interest; *The Spectator*, a journal with conservative views, which publishes articles on many different subjects, including politics; *The New Statesman*, a left-wing periodical containing articles on national and international affairs; *Tribune**, with strongly left-wing political articles and sociological reviews; *New Society*, which has long articles on social matters; *New Scientist*, which reports on scientific matters in language that non-specialists can understand; *Punch*, a long-established humorous magazine which also has serious articles. *The Times* publishes separately a weekly *Educational Supplement*, *Higher Education Supplement* and *Literary Supplement*.

REUTERS

There are a number of news agencies in London, the oldest being Reuters. This was founded in 1851 in London by the German, Julius von Reuter. His service spread and Reuter turned it into a company. It is now owned by newspapers of the United Kingdom, Australia and New Zealand and is used by newspapers all over the world.

FREEDOM OF THE PRESS AND THE PRESS COUNCIL

Newspapers can say what they like about anyone and anything: the army, the Queen, the prime minister, private individuals, the police, the trade unions, provided they say nothing 'libellous' or 'obscene'. Libel is the making of accusations which can be proved to be false and which are harmful to a person's reputation; obscene describes something that shocks because it is improper or in very bad taste. Regarding obscenity, newspapers have very much more freedom now than they had in the early 1960s.

In 1953 the Press Council was established. Among other things, it aims to maintain the established freedom of the press, to maintain its professional standards, to consider complaints about the press and to deal with these complaints in any practical and suitable way.

WRITING TO THE NEWSPAPERS—THE TIMES

Writing to the newspapers and periodicals is a popular pastime for many people. Many women write anxious letters to women's magazines

* The left-wingers of the Labour Party are sometimes known as Tribunites.

LETTERS TO THE EDITOR

The parties and unemployment

From Mr R. G. Opie

Sir, Mr Robert Carr told the Brighton Conference that " It is a matter of historical fact that every Conservative Government has been more successful in controlling unemployment than any Labour Government has been ".

Would Mr ⌐ ⌐ care to name, any single month ⌐ ⌐ Wilson's term of office w⌐ ⌐ wholly un-ⁿploye⌐ ⌐tio⌐

Parting universities and education colleges

From Miss Patricia Higginbotham

Sir, The article by Stephen Jessel (October 14) on colleges of education makes explicit some of the grave issues underlying the suggested possible re-commendations of the James committee.

Irrespective of whether colleges of education are found wanting in their achievements—and there are few institutions which, if put under as strong ⁿicroscope as the colleges have ⁿⁿ not be found wantir ⁿⁿ society—i⌐

economic advantage of this system in his reference to an " easy, cheap and plausible way of meeting the demands for places in higher education ". There is a precedent for this kind of accident in educⁿ⌐ⁿ ⌐ and it has much in common with ⌐

Lowe's revised code of " payment by results " ⁿncing the expenditure ⌐ exchequer whilst ⌐ in the ⌐hew ⌐ⁿ

Complaints against the BBC

From Sir Robert Lusty

Sir, I am sorry to intrude again so soon upon the hospitality of your columns, but wide publicity has been given to an aspect of Mrs Whitehouse's book *Who Does She Think She is ?*, in which she ⌐ ⌐es so-called secret negotiations " ⌐ '66 with the late Lord No ⌐ ⌐en he was Chairⁿ ⌐ ⌐11

Daily Papers Circulation (1976)

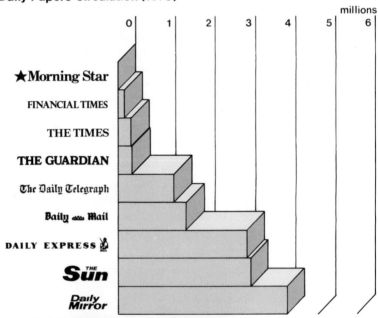

about their marriages. 'My husband used to kiss me good-bye every morning before going to work. He never does now. Does this mean that he no longer loves me?' All such letters are answered. The most interesting—and colourful—are published.

'It's shameful how few playgrounds for children there are in the district where I work,' says Elizabeth. 'I've written letters to *The Guardian* and *The Times* about it.'

Sir Eric writes frequently to *The Times*. Often his letters are for or against some aspect of government policy. If he feels very strongly he sometimes gets other well-known people to sign the letter.

Serious complaints and suggestions, information of all kinds, light-hearted and humorous stories are printed every day in the correspondence columns of *The Times*. People often read the letters before the main news, and the letters do have an influence. Elizabeth's letter may result in more playgrounds, for example.

THESE ARE THE PAPERS THEY MIGHT GET FROM THE NEWSAGENT

THE WILLIAMS: *Daily Express, Daily Mirror, News of the World; Angling Times, Woman's Own.*

JIM: *Motor Cycle, Reveille.*

GARETH: *New Scientist.*

Many working-class Labour supporters, like Gwyn, buy the 'Conservative' *Daily Express*. 'It's got the best football and racing news,' says Gwyn.

BLAKENEY HALL: *The Times, Daily Telegraph, Financial Times, Sunday Times, Sunday Telegraph; Tatler* (society news), *Field* (hunting, shooting, fishing), *Country Life, Illustrated London News, Punch, Naturalist, Birds* and *Country Magazine.*

CHARLES AND ANNE BLAKENEY: *The Times, Financial Times, Sunday Times, Economist, Spectator, Punch, Harpers and Queen* (high-class women's magazine), *Country Life, Fishing, Homes and Gardens, Good Housekeeping.*

MACDONALDS: *Daily Mail, Daily Mirror, Sunday Express, News of the World; Amateur Gardening, Woman, Universe and Catholic Times;* various children's magazines.

Although a Conservative, Ian enjoys *The Mirror*—because it has photographs on most pages. 'I know why he takes *The Mirror*,' says Peggy. 'It's full of pretty girls!'

TOWNSENDS: *Guardian, Sun, Observer, News of the World; Spectator, Listener, New Statesman, New Society, Yachting World, Times Educational Supplement, Spare Rib* (a feminist magazine).

Many intellectuals, like Leonard, read the *News of the World*. 'It's got nothing but sex, violence, and crime!' said Leonard one day. 'Why do you read it then?' asked Elizabeth. 'It amuses me!' replied Leonard.

SUSAN: *Guardian, Observer, Sunday Times*.

JEREMY: *Guardian, Observer, Sunday Times; Private Eye* (humorous, with very biting satires of people in public life), *Poetry Review*.

PENNY: *Daily Express, Sunday Express, News of the World; Woman, Vogue* (high-class fashions).

LISTENING AND VIEWING TASTES[1, 2]

The Williams have the television on most of the time, even when people visit them. They watch anything, usually on ITV. When there is a special programme that Gareth wants to see, a science programme on BBC 2, for example, he escapes to Christine's house. Both he and Christine enjoy listening to pop music on Radio 1.

The Macdonalds watch a lot, usually BBC 1. Peggy rarely misses *Play for Today* and *Panorama*, but both these programmes bore Ian and he usually goes to the pub on those evenings. There are also certain series of plays and serials which they regularly watch together.

Plays in series are complete in themselves, but have the same characters each week and the same background (i.e. police, doctors and hospitals, westerns, etc.). Some are serious, some are comic. Some are imported from the USA, but most are produced in Britain. Serials, on the other hand, are continuous stories which break off at an exciting moment, leaving the viewer waiting and guessing until they are continued at the same time the following week.

'Don't you dare to arrange for us to go out tomorrow, Ian,' said Peggy. 'I simply must know if Elsie and Mick are going to get married. They quarrelled on Wednesday!'

Ian's mother never misses *The Archers*, a daily radio serial about farmers and village life which has been running since 1951.

Susan and Jeremy dislike and scorn television, but they listen frequently to music and serious programmes on the radio. There are also certain 'funny' programmes which they very much enjoy.

Charles and Eric are not regular viewers either, though they watch programmes on sport—a subject which is always extremely well covered.

'There are times when there's sport on every channel!' Hester complains.

Elizabeth Townsend chooses her radio and television programmes very carefully. She has very serious tastes. Both she and Leonard feel that the standard of broadcasting, especially radio, has steadily got worse.

'Once we were the only country in the world which had a whole evening's programme for intellectuals,' said Hester.

'Don't complain too much,' said Carlos. 'You still have some of the best radio programmes I've ever heard.'

Many people, however, are worried by trends in British television. Here is an extract from one of Leonard's radio discussions on the subject. Taking part are Mrs Blackwell, President of the 'Keep Television Clean' movement, Mrs Partridge, a sociologist, and Richard Hunter, a television dramatist.

LEONARD TOWNSEND: Mrs Blackwell objects that there is too much reference to sex on television and that this is a threat to our moral standards. What are your views, Mrs Partridge?

MRS PARTRIDGE: Oh, I think most of the sex on television is pretty harmless, although a lot of it is in bad taste. I'm much more worried about the violence. There are far too many war plays and films, far too many series about secret agents and gangsters and police, and cowboys and Indians—every kind of violence, in fact. I particularly dislike those 'comedy' series in which killing is treated as a joke.

MRS BLACKWELL: Mrs Partridge is quite right. These programmes are disgusting. And so often sex and violence go together in them.

MRS P: I may be old-fashioned, but I do object to the modern TV heroes. A lot of them seem to be no more than professional killers modelled on James Bond. They kill with hardly any conscience at all. They just calmly wipe the blood off their hands and prepare for their next killing.

*An indication of the great variety of programmes which can be seen on television:
historical drama, a very long-running serial, an adaptation of 'War and Peace',
a current affairs programme.*

L.T: Richard Hunter?

RICHARD HUNTER: I think Mrs Partridge is raising an important question here. Ought plays to be a reflection of society, or ought they to try and shape society? As a writer, I naturally feel strongly that artists should be allowed to present life as they see it.

MRS B: It isn't a question of shaping society, Mr Hunter. It's a question of responsibility to the public. Do you realise, for example, the bad influence that some of your plays could have on the young?

R.H: I should be surprised if any of my plays put bad thoughts into the heads of the young! I don't tell them much that they don't know already. Anyway, I've always believed that disguising the truth does more harm than good—to young and old alike.

MRS P: The trouble is we don't see enough plays like yours, Mr Hunter. When you present scenes of sex or violence, you make us think. What I object to is sex and violence used purely for entertainment. Too many programmes treat serious subjects in a trivial way. This can be harmful, I think.

R.H: Triviality can be harmful in itself, surely. So many programmes have no cultural or artistic value whatsoever, childish adventure stories, so-called 'funny' programmes! These programmes aren't about life. They're just a form of escapism, a kind of drug.

L.T: A socially useful drug, perhaps? Aren't we seeing things a bit out of proportion? Any foreigner listening to this programme might get the idea that British television offers nothing but sex, violence and trivialities! Surely this isn't true!

MRS P: No, of course it isn't! We have excellent programmes on the arts and sciences, on social problems and on world affairs. In fact, I doubt if any country has a better television service. But surely we oughtn't to allow standards to fall. I'd like to see the television authorities give way a little less often to the wishes of the majority.

R.H: I agree! But there's a danger here. The television authorities weren't put there to be guardians of our morals, you know. We can't have it both ways. Writers must be allowed to keep their freedom.

NOTES

(1) *The BBC (British Broadcasting Corporation)—Radio and Television*
The BBC is based at Broadcasting House in London, although it has studios in many other parts of the country. It is controlled by a board of governors

appointed by the government, but once appointed this board has complete freedom and the government cannot interfere. Everyone who owns or rents a television set has to pay a yearly licence. There is no advertising on BBC radio or television, and it is from the sale of licences that the BBC gets most of its money. A licence for a black and white set costs £8, and for a colour set £18 a year.

The BBC is not the mouthpiece of the government. On the contrary, it has to be as fair as possible in giving radio and television time to, for example, political parties and religious groups. All three major political parties have equal rights to give political broadcasts, yet each party objects from time to time that the BBC is prejudiced against it.

There are four separate radio channels, each of which 'specialises'. Radio 1 broadcasts mainly pop music. Radio 2 provides light music, comedy programmes, sport. Radio 3 offers serious music, talks on serious subjects and plays of a classical nature. Radio 4 concentrates on the spoken word—i.e. the main news bulletins, talks and discussions, plays etc. There are special programmes for Northern Ireland, Scotland, Wales, and certain parts of England. The BBC has opened local radio stations in a number of large cities and towns. The BBC also broadcasts special programmes about Britain—in forty different languages as well as in English—to all parts of the world.

The BBC has two television channels: BBC1 and BBC2. BBC2 provides a more serious alternative to BBC1, although it also shows films and some comedy. Usually, the same BBC television programmes are seen all over the country, but there are a few variations for local interest. Radio and television programmes are given in the BBC magazine, *The Radio Times*. There is also a weekly magazine, *The Listener*, in which outstanding talks are published.

(2) *ITV (Independent Television)*
There are fifteen different programme companies, each serving a different part of the country. These companies get most of their money from firms who use them for advertising. ITV programmes are interrupted at regular intervals by advertisers. The whole of ITV is controlled by the Independent Broadcasting Authority (IBA). The weekly magazine, *TV Times*, advertises all ITV programmes.

(3) *Rental Services and Colour Sets*
Many people prefer to rent their television sets instead of buying them. The rent for a black and white set is about 80p a week, and sets are repaired free of charge or replaced immediately if they go wrong. The rent of a colour set is more than twice that of a black and white set.

(4) *Commercial Radio*
There are nineteen commercial radio stations in Britain.

QUESTIONS
(1) Ought newspapers to give support—official or unofficial—to political parties?

(2) Do you think that newspapers are 'censored' or controlled in Britain? *Should the Press be controlled?*

(3) In your opinion, do sex and violence—on television, in films or in books—corrupt the young?

(4) There is talk of introducing a second commercial television channel in Britain. Do you agree with this?

FURTHER READING

Martin, K.	Editor
Hoggart, R.	The Uses of Literacy
Rudinger, E. and Kelly, V.	Break for Commercials *(Connexions)*
Groombridge, B.	Television and the People: A Programme for Democratic Participation
Packard, V.	The Hidden Persuaders

There are more than 17 million television sets in Britain.

Of all the sports that people take part in fishing is the most popular ; but football is the most popular of spectator sports.

12

The Sporting British

HOW SPORTING ARE THE BRITISH?

'Many of you British,' said Carlos, 'are more interested in sport than in anything else. I've discovered there's a special telephone number which you can phone during international cricket matches. It gives you the latest score!'

'Yes,' said Anne. 'The British are a very sporting people. They knight their most famous footballers and cricketers. They even knighted the great Australian cricketer, *Sir* Donald Bradman!'

'Doesn't "sporting" have another meaning?' asked Carlos. 'Isn't a man who is "sporting" supposed to believe in "fair play"?'

'You never hear young people use it in that sense now,' said Anne, 'but Charles's father still uses it. He believes that being "sporting" is one of the highest qualities an Englishman can have.'

'It's an old public school tradition,' said Charles. 'It dates from the nineteenth century, when people thought sport developed character and a team spirit. People played just for the love of the game—they were all amateurs. But today, all big sport is professional and top players can make a lot of money. Rugger is an exception of course.⁵'

'Rugger?' said Carlos. 'You mean that terrible game in which you pick the ball up and run with it and the other side tries to knock you down? That's not a game. It's a battle!'

Jeremy hates rugger. He hates all sport, as a result of being forced to play games at school.

'Can you imagine what a waste of time it was, running about a muddy field?' he said to Susan. 'Besides, I was so bad! You have to be good at games to be "somebody" in British schools.'

Games are compulsory in most British schools, although the modern trend is to allow pupils to choose their sport. In many schools, for example, boys no longer have to play cricket.

'There's one advantage in being dressed the way I am,' Jeremy said to Susan. 'It saves me from men who talk sport. They take one look at me and know that I couldn't possibly hold a cricket bat! The Englishman's attitude to sport is so childish. I know a retired schoolmaster who listens all day long to radio commentaries on cricket matches!'

Gareth is not interested in cricket. It bores him, but he likes football and plays for his school team. Christine, too, is good at games. She played tennis for her school, and when she and Gareth play together on the public courts in the park, she usually wins. They are both fond of swimming and sometimes go to the local indoor pool.

Charles Blakeney no longer has time to play serious cricket although he sometimes plays for the village team during weekend visits to Blakeney Hall. His favourite sport is now golf, which he finds useful as well as enjoyable. He has made one or two successful business deals on the golf course. Charles belongs to an expensive club, but men with quite moderate incomes, like Ian Macdonald, for example, can now afford to play golf, because there are many inexpensive clubs and public golf courses too.

There are clubs for practically every sport imaginable. Membership usually costs very little and is sometimes free. Some of these clubs are famous.

'You see that tie Eric is wearing?' Hester said to Carlos. 'It shows he belongs to some sports club or other.'

Many clubs have their own special ties—and blazers.

When the Townsends have time off, they go sailing. The grander name for sailing is 'yachting', but Leonard's boat is too small to be called a yacht. He sails in the Solent, the sheltered water between the Isle of Wight and Southampton. During the summer the river mouths and little harbours around the coast of Britain are crowded with yachts and sailing-boats of all shapes and sizes. Some yachting enthusiasts build their own boats in their backyards and garages.

AT A FOOTBALL MATCH[1]

Gwyn and his mate were entering the stadium. As they passed one of the gates, Gwyn's mate said, 'Look!' A crowd of youths, protesting noisily,

184

were being searched by the police. Bicycle chains and other weapons, including knives, lay in a pile at their feet. Two of the boys were being forced to take off their boots. One of them was Jim.

'The young fool!' said Gwyn. 'I can't do anything with him. It's those gangs.'

'They've got steel tips on them, those boots!' said Gwyn's mate.

They went into the stadium and stood on the terraces behind the goal posts. The ground was packed. There was singing and laughter, and plenty of good-humoured argument between rival supporters.

The match was close. Towards the end tempers became heated, both on the field and among parts of the crowd. A player was sent off for swearing at the referee. Somebody in the crowd threw a beer can onto the field. There were angry shouts, and a fight began. The police moved onto the terraces.

'Hooligans!' said Gwyn. 'Just a few of them, and they spoil it for everyone! They're not interested in the game. Look over there! Did you see that? A kid just got a bicycle chain right across his face.'

Fighting was still going on as Gwyn and his mate returned home. They passed several broken shop windows and they heard the sirens of police cars.

Jim had got home before Gwyn. Mary was bathing his eye, which was red and swollen.

'Two of them went for him!' said Mary.

'Don't ask me to be sorry for him!' said Gwyn. 'He got what he deserved. The fight was all he went for. What was the score, son?'

Jim was silent.

'You see?' said Gwyn. 'He doesn't know and he doesn't care!'

AT A CRICKET MATCH[3]

Last year Charles took an American friend, Culver Jones, to Lord's, the headquarters of English cricket. It was the third day of an international (or Test) match between England and Australia. The large stands around the ground were full of people. The sun was shining. Men were in their shirt sleeves. Their wives or girlfriends were unpacking picnic baskets. People were also sitting on the grass inside the white boundary line.

'That Englishman who's bowling—that means throwing the ball—'

Charles said to Culver, 'is trying to hit those three sticks, called a "wicket". The Australian with the bat is trying to protect his wicket and at the same time hit the ball far enough so that he can run to the other wicket. That's how his side scores. It's the number of runs between the wickets which counts.'

'Oh!' said Culver.

The crowd watched in silence. Occasionally there was a little burst of clapping. After a while Culver looked at his watch.

'We've been here for ten minutes,' he said, 'and the two batsmen have only run once. And what about all those other players on the field? They just seem to be standing around doing nothing!'

Charles started to explain, but he soon gave up.

'It's too complicated,' he said. 'It takes years to learn to play the game, and unless you've been brought up with it, you can't really understand it.'

Culver fell asleep. Suddenly he was woken by a great roar. The crowd was on its feet. They were cheering excitedly.

'He's out!' Charles said. 'Their best batsman! Look! The ball has hit the wicket!'

'Oh!' said Culver.

A new batsman came in. The crowd settled down again. Every two or three minutes there was a mild burst of clapping. Some of the women were reading magazines or sleeping. The men were chatting and drinking beer from cans. Only the little boys made any noise.

'It's so slow!' said Culver. 'Only the English could have invented such a game. No wonder so few countries play it!'

'It's played all over the Commonwealth,' said Charles. 'And it's not always slow, quiet and unexciting. When the West Indian team is playing, the West Indians in the crowd cheer, shout and give advice at every ball. In fact, they make as much noise as a football crowd. Cricket is much more popular in the West Indies than football.'

'Are the West Indians good at cricket?'

'They're amongst the best. Many of them come over here during the summer and play for professional English clubs. So do Australians, Indians, Pakistanis—and a lot of South Africans as well.'

'But how did they learn the game?'

'We taught it to them—in our colonial days! In fact, if you Americans hadn't revolted so early, we'd have taught *you* the game!'

HORSE RACING, HUNTING AND RIDING

Every Saturday Gwyn goes round to the betting-shop and puts 25p on a
100 to 1 outsider, that is, on a horse that nobody expects to win. He then
goes home to watch the race on television. He won £50 once, but
usually his horse comes in last. Gwyn loves a gamble, but he never *goes*
to the races—not like Sir Eric and Charles Blakeney, who, once a year,
put on their top hats and tail coats and go to Ascot, the most fashionable
of all race meetings[6].

Hester and Anne go with their husbands. Ascot is an important
social occasion. The Queen always opens the meeting by driving down
the race course in an open carriage, and everybody who enters the
Royal Enclosure must be correctly dressed.

'It's more like a fashion show than a race meeting,' said Anne.
'People seem much more interested in the hats and dresses of the women
than in the horses!'

The Blakeneys do not go hunting[9], but their neighbour, George
Blandford, is master of the local foxhounds (dogs which hunt foxes and
deer are always called 'hounds'). George has a stable of fine hunters
(hunting horses). His 'hunt' is not as fashionable as the famous hunts in
the midlands and west country, but he and his fellow huntsmen wear
the traditional red coats and black caps.

Susan is not very popular with the Blandfords, because she belongs to
the Anti-Blood Sports League. She and about twenty of her young
friends once lay down across the road in front of the Blandfords' stables
just before a hunt, and there were not enough local policemen to move
them.

However, Susan herself loves riding and keeps a pony of her own at
Blakeney Hall. Many young people ride, and those who cannot afford
to own ponies hire them from riding stables. Christine, for example,
spent a holiday pony-trekking in Scotland.

FISHING

Gwyn is an angler. Of all the sports that people take an active part in,
angling is the most popular one in Britain. Most Sunday afternoons
Gwyn and his friends go to a muddy canal in north-east London. There
they sit for hours beside their rods and wait for the fish to bite the worms
on the hooks. They do not often take any fish home to their wives. They

usually throw them back alive into the canal. However, they like to boast about the size, weight and number of the fish which they catch, and Gwyn has won several angling competitions.

Charles is not an angler. He fishes for salmon in the mountain rivers of Scotland, and he uses an artificial fly which he throws on to the surface of the water. Fly-fishing needs skill, and to Anne's disappointment, Charles often returns home without having caught any salmon at all. Whatever his catch, he pays a high fee to the owner of the river for the right to fish there.

Gwyn, however, pays nothing for his day's fishing.

SHOOTING[9]

Farmers shoot on their own land, but otherwise shooting (i.e. hunting with a gun) in Britain is mainly a rich man's sport—practised in the woods of country estates and on the moors of Scotland and northern England. Many of these moors are privately owned and reserved for

Two aspects of cricket:
fans invading the pitch
at a Test match between
England and the West Indies.

game. Apart from game, few birds or animals are shot for pleasure in Britain. Many birds are, in fact, protected, and anyone shooting them can be prosecuted.

Susan does not like shooting any more than she likes hunting and she finds it very difficult to understand her father's attitude.

'You're a member of the Wild Life Preservation Society, Father,' she said one day to Sir Eric. 'Pheasants are wild birds. Yet you raise them in your own woods—just for the fun of shooting at them! And you think it's fair because you only shoot at them when they're flying.'

'Well, at least it gives the bird a chance!' said Sir Eric. 'Besides, you know how I feel about birds. I don't just go out and shoot at anything anywhere, as they do in some countries.'

Village cricket—a familiar scene on a Sunday afternoon in summer.

NOTES

(1) Association Football (*popularly called 'soccer'*)

Football is much the most popular team game in Britain and the chief winter game for boys in most schools. There is no 'British' team; England, Scotland, Wales and Northern Ireland compete separately in European and World Cup matches.

English and Welsh professional clubs play against each other in a league with four divisions. The Scottish League has a Premier Division and a First Division. The champion club of the English and Welsh First Division and of the Scottish Premier Division compete *separately* in the European Cup competition.

As well as league football, there is a knock-out 'Cup' competition between *all* the English and Welsh clubs, including amateur clubs. The 'Cup Final' is played in May at Wembley Stadium in London and excites immense enthusiasm.

(2) Football Pools

'Doing the pools' is a popular form of betting on football results each week. It is possible to win more than half a million pounds for a few pence. There is no equivalent form of betting on cricket, so during the summer months people bet on the results of Australian football.

(3) Cricket

This is called the English 'national' game and it is the chief summer game for boys in most schools. The first class professional cricket clubs represent counties and play three-day matches against one another. But since the war these matches have become less and less popular. They tend to be slow and often end with no result. Cricket was said to be dying. Then Sunday half-day league matches were introduced, so arranged that there had to be a winner. There were also one-day Cup matches, with the final at Lord's (see below). People began to flock to the cricket grounds again. The excitement at the Cup final match is tremendous. In 1975 the Sportsman of the Year was a cricketer. There is still great interest in the five-day international matches, called Test matches. These are played between England, Australia, West Indies, Pakistan, India and New Zealand. None of these countries play against South Africa, because of its government's racialist policies. Cricket is a Commonwealth and *English* game. There are no first class clubs in Scotland or Ireland, and only one in Wales. There are a large number of amateur clubs all over England.

(4) The MCC

The Marylebone Cricket Club has its headquarters at Lord's, in the Marylebone district of London. Lord's cricket ground is the best known of all the cricket grounds in the world. The MCC was established in 1789 and published the first set of laws for cricket. For this reason it has remained the ruling authority in cricket affairs and chooses the English team (consisting of eleven players with an extra 'twelfth man') to play in Test matches.

(5) *Rugby Union Football* (popularly called 'rugger')
This is the chief winter game in most public and some L.E.A. schools. However, with the increasing popularity of soccer, many schools that formerly played only rugger now play soccer as well.

England, Scotland, Wales, Ireland (combining Eire and Ulster players) and France compete in a yearly championship. The world's toughest and most enthusiastic rugby countries are South Africa and New Zealand. Rugby Union is a strictly amateur game, and a player who accepts any form of reward for playing may be forbidden to play the game again. Rugby Union is also played in Fiji, Tonga, Argentina, Rumania and Japan.

There is a professional form of the game called Rugby League, which has only thirteen players (instead of fifteen) and slightly different rules. Rugby League is also played in other parts of the world, particularly in France, New Zealand and Australia. It is generally considered a tougher game than soccer and it was from rugby football that American football developed.

(6) *Famous (Horse) Race Meetings*
The Grand National is England's principal steeplechase, that is, a race over fences and ditches. It takes place in March or April at Aintree, near Liverpool. The course is over four miles long and includes thirty jumps, of which fourteen are jumped twice. Many horses do not finish and many people think it is too dangerous.

The Derby is the leading English flat race (no jumps). It takes place in May or June at Epsom, near London.

The Ascot Races are held in June at Ascot, six miles from Windsor. The meeting is noted for its fashions, particularly women's hats, many of which are made specially for the Ascot meeting.

Goodwood Races are held during the last week of July at Goodwood, in Sussex. It is another fashionable meeting, though not to the same extent as Ascot.

(7) *Other Well-known Sporting Events*
The Boat Race, meaning the Oxford and Cambridge University boat race, is rowed at Easter time over a course four and a half miles long on the River Thames, in London. Crowds line the banks to watch the race, and thousands more watch it on television.

The Open Lawn Tennis Championships are held in July at Wimbledon in London. Most tennis players regard the Wimbledon tournament (competition) as the world championship. The whole tournament is covered by television, but large numbers of people queue all night outside the grounds in order to be able to get tickets for the finals.

The Open Golf Championship. Golf was invented by the Scots, and its headquarters is at the Royal and Ancient Golf Club, St. Andrews.

The Oxford and Cambridge University Rugby Match is held at Twickenham, London, the headquarters of British Rugby Union. More than 50,000 people watch this match every year and it is televised.

The Henley (Rowing) Regatta is an annual amateur event in which a number of teams from other countries also take part. Henley is an attractive summer resort on the Thames, in Oxfordshire. The regatta is a fashionable event.

Cowes Week is a yachting regatta. Cowes is a small town on the Isle of Wight, opposite Southampton, and a world-famous yachting centre.

(8) *British Successes in Major Sports* (since 1945)

Football: England won the World Cup in 1966; Celtic (Scottish club) won the European Cup in 1967, Manchester United in 1968; Tottenham Hotspur won the European Cup Winner's Cup in 1963, West Ham United in 1965, Rangers in 1968, Manchester City in 1970 and Chelsea in 1971. The European Fairs Cup was won by Newcastle United in 1969, Arsenal in 1970 and Leeds United in 1968 and 1971. Tottenham Hotspur won the UEFA Cup in 1972, Liverpool won it in 1973.

Tennis: Angela Mortimer beat Christine Truman in the ladies' final at Wimbledon in 1961 — the only all-British final since the war. Ann Jones beat the American, Billie-Jean King, in the 1969 final, Virginia Wade won the US Ladies Open Championship in 1968, and the Australian Ladies Open Championship in 1972.

Grand Prix Motor Racing: There have been eight British world champions since the championship was begun in 1951.

Olympic Games: Gold medals have been won by Britons as follows — London (1948), 1; Helsinki (1952), 1; Melbourne (1956), 6; Rome (1960), 2; Tokyo (1964), 4; Mexico (1968), 5; Munich (1972, 4; Montreal (1976), 3.

Golf: Tony Jacklin won both the British and American Open Golf Championships in the same year (1969–70).

Rugby Union: In 1971 the British Lions (a combined touring team from England, Ireland, Scotland and Wales) beat New Zealand for the first time ever. In 1974 the Lions beat the South Africans in South Africa for the first time, not losing a single match. The Lions toured South Africa in spite of the British government's objections.

(9) *Hunting and Shooting*

There are 'close seasons', when it is unlawful to shoot or hunt game or deer and certain other animals. These seasons vary, depending on the animals concerned. There is no law about hunting foxes, but there is a fox-hunting season — from November to March. In the Scottish Highlands deer are hunted on foot, with a gun. This is called 'deer stalking'.

QUESTIONS

(1) Do you think it is a good idea to have compulsory games at school, or do you agree with Jeremy's strong disapproval?

(2) How do you explain violence at football matches?

(3) Sir Eric Blakeney believes that the playing of team games has helped to

make the British what they are. Do you think that sport plays an important part
in character-building?
(4) Do you think that international sport helps to bring nations closer together,
or do you think it pushes them further apart?

FURTHER READING

Gillett, C.   All in the Game *(Connexions)*
Glanville, B.   The Puffin Book of Football
Storey, D.   This Sporting Life (F)

*Ascot is as much a fashion show as a race meeting, and traditionally extravagant hats are
a very important feature.*

An auction of old masters
at Sotheby's.

Alan Ayckbourn, one of Britain's
most successful playwrights,
once had five different plays
running in London theatres at
the same time. His plays are
extremely funny, but they also
criticise English middle-class
marriage and suburban ambitions.

13
The Arts

It is impossible in a book of this kind to cover such an immense subject. This chapter does no more than suggest trends and give some idea of the atmosphere in which modern British writers, artists and musicians work. A selection of names can be found at the end of each section, and in the notes. Apart from one small exception, the imaginary characters have not been introduced into this chapter.

Since the second world war there have been great changes in literature and in the arts. These changes have much to do with the breaking down of social barriers and the improvement of education. Wider education has made young people from every social background conscious of the arts, and has awakened their interest in them. The pop revolution of the 1960s (see p. 204) also did much to bring a new vigour to the world of art, literature and music. It encouraged members of the younger generation to express their thoughts and feelings, and it hastened a break with the traditions of the past. Today, artists, musicians and writers have a much wider public than they had before the war. Far more people now read books and go to the theatre, concerts and picture galleries.

NOVELS[2] AND PLAYS[3]

Between the two world wars, serious novelists and playwrights were read and appreciated mainly by people from middle and upper-class backgrounds, for these people had money and this gave them opportunities for education and leisure which were beyond the reach of the poorer classes. For the same reason, the writers tended to come from the same kind of background, although there were many exceptions. The novelist, D. H. Lawrence, for example, was the son of a miner. But Lawrence's books were bought and read by middle-class readers, and the language which he used was literary, rather than popular.

Lawrence, like other writers of the 1920s and 1930s — Aldous Huxley, H. G. Wells, and the older men, George Bernard Shaw and John Galsworthy — was presenting his public with his own view of life. He was hoping to persuade his readers to think like himself. Many of the serious writers of the period were concerned with social and political problems. Their plays and novels were full of arguments in favour of social reforms. They made amusing and often bitter comments on the injustices and absurdities of life — especially middle-class life. The novelist, Evelyn Waugh, called one of his novels *Vile Bodies* (vile means extremely ugly and unpleasant). Some novelists gave horrible warnings about the kind of future that mankind might have to face. Huxley's amusing *Brave New World* and Orwell's frightening *Nineteen Eighty-Four* (written in the 1940s) are still taken very seriously by many young people today.

Other writers, like Virginia Woolf and the Irishman, James Joyce, were more interested in thoughts and feelings than in social life, and they expressed their thoughts in a language which was sometimes extremely difficult to understand. Playwrights, too, experimented with language. In the late 1930s and in the 1940s T. S. Eliot and Christopher Fry wrote serious plays in verse. At the same time there were plenty of novelists and playwrights whose only aim was to excite, to amuse and to move to tears! The most popular and successful of these writers was Noel Coward. Not surprisingly, people tended to divide writers into two kinds — serious, or intellectual, and light, or non-intellectual.

Then, in the 1950s, a literary revolution took place. A new kind of literature burst upon the scene. The writers of this new literature — Kingsley Amis, John Wain, John Braine, John Osborne, Arnold Wesker and Alan Sillitoe — became known as the 'Angry Young Men'. They came from working-class and lower middle-class backgrounds, and they tended to be left-wing. They wrote about the ugly and sordid realities of life as they knew it, and they wrote 'angrily'. John Osborne called his first play *Look Back in Anger*.

These new novels and plays were not written in literary or

intellectual language, but in the ordinary and sometimes ugly language of daily life. The scene was often set in the dark back rooms and kitchens of northern industrial cities. The 'heroes' were not usually men with ideas or ideals. More often they were bitter, weak men, defeated by the small dramas and miseries of everyday life.

Here are the thoughts of the working-class hero of John Braine's novel, *Room at the Top*, as he watches a smart young man climb into a smart car (an Aston Martin) beside a smart young woman:

'He hadn't ever had to work for anything he wanted: it had all been given to him. The salary I had been so pleased about, an increase from grade ten to grade nine, would seem a pittance to him. The suit in which I fancied myself so much—my best suit—would seem cheap and nasty to him. He wouldn't *have* a "best" suit: all his clothes would be "best".'

'For the moment I hated him ... I tasted the sourness of envy ... I wanted an Aston Martin ... I wanted a girl with a Riviera suntan. These were my rights, I felt ...'

Many people were shocked by the violence of these young writers, who scorned so many social and literary traditions. But their talent was soon recognised by the critics, by the younger generation and even by the intellectuals, for they had something new to say. Their writing was often deliberately anti-intellectual, and yet they forced people to think.

Some of these writers of the 1950s and early 1960s are no longer as left-wing as they were. Some of them, like Kingsley Amis and John Braine, have even moved to the right. The writers of the 1970s come from an infinite variety of backgrounds, and today one no longer asks from what background a writer comes. The ugliness and meanness of life remains a favourite subject for novels and stage plays, as well as for films and television plays. The writers of today are interested in the small details of life. They like to show what goes on beneath the surface, whether it be in private or family life, or in factories, big business, offices, universities, and even in sport. A successful playwright and novelist of the 1960s and 1970s, David Storey, wrote his first novel about an incident in the life of a professional rugby league player (see p. 191). Most modern writers are observers rather than commentators.

Some writers, among them Iris Murdoch, William Golding, Lawrence Durrell, Muriel Spark, do more than observe. They explore the reasons why people act as they do. These writers are perhaps following in the path of Virginia Woolf and other writers of the 1920s and 1930s. William Golding's deeply disturbing novel, *Lord of the Flies*, symbolises the cruelty of human society, although outwardly it is about the relationships and rivalries of little boys. Most modern novelists and playwrights, however, are simply looking at life and making few comments.

Harold Pinter, perhaps the most distinctive playwright of the 1960s and 1970s, claims that he has no social or symbolic message. He says that he only puts down what he sees, and that people can read into his plays and sketches what they like.

Pinter's characters are ordinary people, living simple, unexciting lives. Their conversations are completely unintellectual, and sometimes they hardly talk at all. When they do speak they want to be listened to, but they do not want to listen. Most of them have one thing in common. They cannot communicate with one another, that is, they cannot understand each other's thoughts and feelings. They are lonely and unhappy.

Whatever Pinter may say about himself, many people feel that his plays are symbolic of the loneliness of modern man.

POETS[4]

Poetry is one of the more popular arts among young people today. School children, university students, young working-class boys and girls write poetry and read it to one another in poetry clubs. There are also public poetry readings—in small hired rooms and even in big concert halls. Modern young poets give live performances and need an audience almost as much as musicians do. Some of this poetry is published in book form by small, private, non profit-making printing presses. It is sometimes direct, sometimes symbolic. But whatever its form it expresses a feeling for the realities of life—a dissatisfaction with society, a hatred of war, materialism, racialism and class, a longing for universal love. Some of it has been accepted by the big publishers and is bought and read—not only by young people, but by many older people as well. The pop revolution has had a great influence on poetry. A group of young working-class poets from Liverpool have made a name for themselves nationally and are now known as the Mersey Poets.

We have lost interest in wars and political situations,
There are craters in our hearts,
We must not neglect them.
Let the pink bird sing.

(From a poem by Brian Patten, one of the leading Mersey Poets)

'When in public, poetry should take off its clothes and wave to the nearest person in sight,' said Brian Patten. 'It should be seen in the company of thieves and lovers rather than that of journalists and publishers.'

THE 'ALTERNATIVE' MOVEMENT

There was an 'Underground' Movement in the sixties which performed daring morality plays in private clubs and theatres. It was anti-Establishment (see Chapter 1, Note 3) and anti-party politics. It produced periodicals which were not sold by the booksellers. There is now a new anti-Establishment movement—the 'Alternative' Movement. It is interested in the simple life, with uncomplicated machines and health food. There are no leaders and no one seeks to lead. The followers call themselves 'anarchists', but are completely non-violent. They produce magazines. There is a periodical called 'Peace News', and others on health foods and alternative technology. These journals are accepted by booksellers.

FILMS

The British cinema, too, is experimenting with new ideas. Directors like Tony Richardson, Joseph Losey (born in USA), Lindsay Anderson, Ken Loach, Ken Russell, have made films about the social and moral problems of the day. Their best films are both good entertainment and works of art, and they often ask questions which excite the younger generation and disturb their elders. Many small provincial cinemas have closed down because of the rivalry of television, but in the cities, especially in London, the cinemas are often full. Most of the best foreign films are also shown in London and attract large audiences.

PAINTERS[5] AND SCULPTORS[6]

There is probably a greater interest in painting and sculpture today than ever before. Artists are experimenting with colours and shapes and materials of all kinds. They hold exhibitions on street pavements, in parks, in empty buildings, as well as in schools, universities and art clubs. If they are lucky, their works are chosen for exhibition by the Institution of Contemporary (present-day) Art, which was founded to help young artists. Some art lovers do not consider this work to be 'art' at all, but many people like it, because it is concerned with things and experiences of everyday life.

A few young painters and sculptors have been very successful and have had their work accepted by well-known London art galleries. A very few have become rich. The pop artist, David Hockney, for example, has sold pictures for thousands of pounds. Most artists, however, make practically no money at all.

The older generation of modern painters, such as John Piper and Graham Sutherland, now have an international reputation, but in their youth they offended traditionalists. Henry Moore startled people when he first exhibited his sculptures. Today, in his old age, he is accepted as one of the world's greatest living sculptors.

CRAFTSMEN

An interest in crafts of all kinds has grown up again. In schools, colleges and evening classes (see p. 164) more and more young people are learning crafts—pottery, wood-carving, furniture-making and metal work. Potters have opened shops in towns and villages all over the country, and English hand-made pottery is being exported abroad. Many shops also sell hand-woven and hand-printed cloth, and hand-made jewellery.

ART COLLECTIONS[7, 8]

The English have always been great art collectors. In the eighteenth and nineteenth centuries the aristocracy, country gentlemen and businessmen, filled their houses with valuable paintings, furniture and ornaments which they brought back from their travels abroad. Their collections can be seen today in museums, and in country houses, palaces and castles which are open to the public. During the nineteenth century the state itself became a collector. There are museums and picture galleries in most cities. It is claimed that the London galleries and museums hold a richer variety of works of art than any other city in the world.

London is also the world's most important art market. Art treasures from every country and every century pass through the sale rooms of the famous art auctioneers, Sotheby's and Christies.

MUSIC (Notes 10 to 15)

In the sixteenth and seventeenth centuries English musicians had a great reputation in Europe, both for their talent and for their originality. Today there is a revival of interest in these neglected composers. It was their experiments in keyboard music which helped to form the base from which grew most of the great harpsichord and piano music of the seventeenth, eighteenth and nineteenth centuries. William Byrd was the most distinguished English composer of this time, and his name is still widely known.

In the centuries which followed England produced no composers of world rank except for Purcell in the seventeenth and eighteenth centuries, and Elgar in the twentieth century. Some people, it is true, claim that the German-born Handel (1685–1759) was English. Handel became an English subject, and he lived and worked for much of his life in London. His world famous oratorio, *Messiah*, was composed to English words. He was loved and admired by all English music lovers of his day. He is still extremely popular, but he cannot really be called an English composer.

Today, however, many people believe that there has been a re-flowering of English music, and that the compositions of some contemporary composers will live on after their deaths. The music of Michael Tippett, Benjamin Britten and William Walton is performed all over the world.

Benjamin Britten is not modern in the musical sense of the word, but he is modern in his attitude towards his public. He has been called a 'people's composer' because he has composed music, particularly operas and choral works, that can be sung by ordinary people and by children. Some of his operas, such as *Noyes Fludde* (Noah's Flood) are performed in churches every year, and people from the surrounding countryside sing and act in them. The festival which he started in his little home town, Aldeburgh, on the North Sea coast of Suffolk, has become one of the most important musical festivals in Britain.

Benjamin Britten's music, however, is traditional compared with the works of many of the younger generation of composers, whose experiments are now having a considerable influence abroad. Young British composers, like Peter Maxwell Davies, Richard Rodney Bennett and John Tavener, now have an international reputation.

It is significant that Richard Rodney Bennett is a very fine trumpeter and once played the piano in a jazz band, for the dividing lines between serious music on the one hand and jazz, pop and folk music on the other, are becoming less and less clear, and the influence that they are having on one another is increasing.

Significantly, too, the most popular instrument among young people today is the guitar. Some young people carry their guitars with them wherever they go. They join together in folk evenings, and there they play and sing both traditional and modern folk music.

Many twentieth-century British composers, including Vaughan Williams, Tippett and Britten, have been attracted and influenced by old English folk songs. But modern folk music has a different sense. Although the tunes follow the traditional style, the rhythms are very up-to-date, and the words often have a strong social message.

However, it was not an Englishman, but an American, Bob Dylan, who started the fashion for modern folk music. Dylan composes, writes and sings his own songs. His famous protest song, *Blowing in the Wind*, which criticises so bitterly man's cruelty to man, shows how effectively poetry and music can be married. Bob Dylan's influence in shaping the new pop culture has been very great.

DO THE ENGLISH LISTEN TO MUSIC?

There are concert halls in most of the big cities, and in London there are opportunities for listening to music unequalled in any other city in the world—as Culver Jones discovered when he went to a booking agency in the West End.

CULVER JONES: Have you any tickets for the Festival Hall tonight?

GIRL: Which concert, sir?

CULVER: Is there more than one?

GIRL: Yes, sir. There's a symphony concert with the Royal Philharmonic Orchestra in the *main* Festival Hall. There's a chamber concert with the Amadeus Quartet in the Queen Elizabeth Hall next door, and there's a concert of Indian music in the Purcell Room—

that's in the same building as the Queen Elizabeth Hall.

CULVER: Well! Well! Is that all you've got to offer me?

GIRL: Oh no, sir! There's a Promenade Concert with the BBC Orchestra at the Royal Albert Hall—

CULVER: Promenade Concert? What's that?

GIRL: Well, sir, it's a kind of concert where you have to stand—if you want a really cheap ticket, that is. Promenade tickets cost only 30 pence*, but if you want one you'll have to start queuing this afternoon. Promenading is really for young people, sir.

CULVER: Then it's not for me!

GIRL: There are seats upstairs, sir, but they're more expensive and I'm afraid they're all booked out for this evening. Perhaps you'd like to go to the Wigmore Hall? There's a recital there by a new English tenor.

CULVER: No, I don't think so—

GIRL: Well, there's opera, of course[15]. There's Verdi's *Falstaff* at the Royal Opera House at Covent Garden—with an international cast—or there's Benjamin Britten's *Midsummer Night's Dream* at Sadler's Wells.[15] It's *very* good, they say. Are you staying in England long, sir?

CULVER: About six months.

GIRL: Well, sir, if you're really fond of music, perhaps you'd like to do a little trip around Britain visiting all the festivals.[11] Here's a list with all the dates. Just write, or give me a ring.

HOW MUSICAL ARE THE BRITISH?

'Wherever I go in your country,' said Culver, 'I find small groups of people, young and old, who get together to make music. They play in quartets or small orchestras. They sing in choirs or in opera groups. And, like so many of your amateur drama groups, they often play before large and enthusiastic audiences.'

There are amateur orchestras, choirs and opera groups even in small country towns. Many schools, too, now have orchestras. Their best players are chosen to play in the county youth orchestras, and a few of the very best may be picked for the National Youth Orchestra. The NYO is trained by distinguished conductors. It plays in the Festival Hall and in other big concert halls, and it travels abroad. Some of the county youth orchestras also give concerts abroad.

* £1 in 1976.

Even if the word 'pop' disappears from the English vocabulary, the influence of pop will remain. Pop has become part of British—and American—history.

There has always been a close cultural link, or tie, between Britain and English-speaking America, not only in literature but also in the popular arts, especially music. Before the second world war the Americans exported jazz and the blues. During the 1950s they exported rock 'n' roll, and star singers like Elvis Presley were idolised by young Britons and Americans alike.

Then in the early 1960s a new sound was heard, very different from anything which had so far come from the American side of the Atlantic. This was the Liverpool, or Merseyside, 'beat'. Situated on the River Mersey in the north-western corner of the industrial Black Country, Liverpool was not a place which anyone visited for fun. Until the 1960s it was known only as one of Britain's largest ports. Then, almost overnight, it became world famous as the birthplace of the new pop culture which, in a few years, swept across Britain and America, and across most of the countries of the western world.

The people responsible for the pop revolution were four Liverpool boys who joined together in a group and called themselves The Beatles. They played in small clubs in the back streets of the city. Unlike the famous solo stars who had their songs written for them, the Beatles wrote their own words and music. They had a close personal relationship with their audience, and they expected them to join in and dance to the 'beat' of the music. Audience participation is an essential characteristic of pop culture.

Some pop groups, in particular the Rolling Stones, did more than just entertain. They wrote words which were deliberately intended to shock. They represented the anger and bitterness of youth struggling for freedom against authority, and for this reason they were regarded by some people as the personification of the 'permissive society'.

The Beatles, on the other hand, finally won the affection—and admiration—of people of all ages and social backgrounds. As they developed, their songs became more serious. They wrote not only of love, but of death and old age and poverty and daily life. They were respected by many intellectuals and by some serious musicians. Largely thanks to the Beatles, pop music has grown into an immense and profitable industry.

In 1970–71 the partnership of the Beatles broke up. They still write and record songs separately, but whatever happens to their music, the Beatles will surely have a permanent place in the social history of Britain.

The influence of British pop in America was immense. American pop groups soon became as famous as British groups. Both British and Americans are experimenting with new ideas, and pop is developing and changing, and merging with modern folk music.

NOTES

(1) *Arts Council*: This body was established in 1946 to improve knowledge, understanding and practice of the arts. Members are appointed by the Secretary of State for Education and Science. The Council organises exhibitions and gives advice and money grants to authors, artists, musicians, theatre and opera companies, etc.

(2) *A Selection of Novelists*
1920–50: James Joyce (d. 1941), Aldous Huxley (d. 1963), H. G. Wells (d. 1946), D. H. Lawrence (d. 1930), Evelyn Waugh (d. 1966), Virginia Woolf (d. 1941), George Orwell (d. 1950), Somerset Maugham (d. 1965), J. B. Priestley,

Graham Greene, Elizabeth Bowen (d. 1973), Anthony Powell, E. M. Forster (d. 1970), John Galsworthy (d. 1933).

Younger Generation—active since 1950: Kingsley Amis, John Braine, John Wain, Alan Sillitoe, Angus Wilson, William Golding, Iris Murdoch, Lawrence Durrell, Muriel Spark, Henry Green, William Cooper, C. P. Snow, Edna O'Brien, Doris Lessing (born in Rhodesia), Margaret Drabble, Elizabeth Taylor, Olivia Manning, Elizabeth Jane Howard, Stan Barstow, David Storey, L. P. Hartley (d. 1972), John Fowles.

(3) *A Selection of Playwrights*

1920–50: G. B. Shaw (d. 1950), John Galsworthy (d. 1933), Sean O'Casey (Irish writer of symbolic plays about the miseries of Irish life—d. 1964), J. B. Priestley, Noel Coward (light comedies—d. 1973), T. S. Eliot (born in USA but lived in England—d. 1965), Christopher Fry, W. H. Auden (d. 1973) and Christopher Isherwood, Somerset Maugham (d. 1965).

Younger Generation—active since 1950: Samuel Beckett (Irish writer, living in France, who usually writes his plays in French), John Osborne, Arnold Wesker, Joe Orton (d. 1967), David Mercer, John Whiting (d. 1963), Brendan Behan (d. 1964), Shelagh Delaney, Giles Cooper (d. 1966), Harold Pinter, Robert Bolt, Christopher Hampton, Alun Owen, Henry Livings, David Storey, John Mortimer, Tom Stoppard, Peter Shaffer, John Arden, Edward Bond, Alan Ayckbourn.

(4) *A Selection of Poets*

1920–50: W. B. Yeats (Irish poet—d. 1939), A. E. Housman (d. 1936), Walter de la Mare (d. 1956), John Masefield (d. 1967), Edith Sitwell (d. 1964), Robert Graves, T. S. Eliot (d. 1965), Louis MacNeice (d. 1963), W. H. Auden (d. 1973), Cecil Day-Lewis (d. 1976), Kathleen Raine, Edwin Muir, William Empson, Dylan Thomas (d. 1953), Stevie Smith (d. 1971).

Younger Generation—active since 1950: Ted Hughes, Thom Gunn, Sylvia Plath (d. 1963), Philip Larkin, George MacBeth, Brian Patten and Roger McGough (Mersey Poets), Seamus Heaney, Jon Stallworthy, Robert Conquest, Donald Davie, Elizabeth Jennings, Lawrence Durrell, D. J. Enright, Peter Redgrove, Philip Hobsbaum, John Betjeman.

(5) *A Selection of Painters*

1920–50: Augustus John (d. 1961), William Nicholson (d. 1949), Stanley Spencer (d. 1959), L. S. Lowry (d. 1976), Christopher Wood (d. 1930), Paul Nash (d. 1946), John Nash, Ben Nicholson, Graham Sutherland, John Piper.

Younger Generation—active since 1950: Victor Pasmore, Francis Bacon, Bridget Riley, David Hockney, John Hoyland, Richard Hamilton, Richard Smith.

(6) *A Selection of Sculptors*

1920–50: Jacob Epstein (d. 1959), Frank Dobson (d. 1962), Henry Moore, Barbara Hepworth (d. 1975).

Younger Generation—active since 1950: Elizabeth Frink, Anthony Caro, Philip King, Reg Butler, Lynn Chadwick, Eduardo Paolozzi.

(7) *Museums and Picture Galleries of London*
Museums: British Museum, Victoria and Albert Museum, London Museum, Natural History Museum, Science Museum, National Maritime Museum.

(8) *Galleries*: National Gallery, National Portrait Gallery, Tate Gallery, Wallace Collection, Queen's collection at Buckingham Palace, Hayward Gallery (for art exhibitions), Institute of Contemporary Art (modern art exhibitions of all kinds), Royal Academy (for special exhibitions).

(9) *The Theatre*: There are 200 professional companies in Britain and many excellent theatres, some new, in provincial cities and towns. There is a festival theatre at Chichester, Sussex (season May to August). But London is the theatrical centre. There are thirty theatres in the West End. The National Theatre Company used to perform at the Old Vic and has now moved to the new National Theatre on the South Bank of the Thames. It also tours the provinces. The Royal Shakespeare Company performs at the Aldwych Theatre in London and at the Shakespeare Memorial Theatre at Stratford-on-Avon (season April to December). The Royal Court and Mermaid Theatres in London put on modern plays. Very modern plays can be seen at the Roundhouse in Camden Town.

Amateur Theatres: There are enthusiastic groups in every town, large and small. In few other countries is the interest in amateur theatricals so great.

The National Youth Theatre, whose members are all young people, produces plays at home and abroad during the summer.

(10) *A Selection of Composers*
1920–50: Edward Elgar (d. 1934), Ralph Vaughan Williams (d. 1958), Arthur Bliss (d. 1975), William Walton, Benjamin Britten, Michael Tippett, Malcolm Arnold.

Younger Generation—active since 1950: John Tavener, John McCabe, Tim Souster, Alexander Goehr, Elizabeth Lutyens, Peter Maxwell Davies, Richard Rodney Bennett, Humphrey Searle.

(11) *A few of the most important Festivals of Music, Drama (theatre) and the Arts*: Edinburgh (August to September), Aldeburgh (June), Bath (June), Cheltenham (July), King's Lynn (August), Royal National Eisteddfod of Wales (August), International Eisteddfod at Llangollen (July), Three Choirs Festival—in cathedrals of Gloucester, Worcester and Hereford in turn (August).

Promenade Season (London, mid-July to mid-September) every night a great variety of orchestras and conductors, both British and foreign.

(12) *First-Class Orchestras*: BBC, London Symphony, London Philharmonic, Royal Philharmonic, New Philharmonia (all based in London); The Hallé (Manchester), City of Birmingham, Bournemouth, Royal Liverpool Philharmonic, Scottish National.

There are a number of first-class string and chamber orchestras and several chamber music groups of international fame.

(13) *Choral Singing* is a speciality of the British, and there are excellent choral societies in many cities, e.g. The Huddersfield Choral Society.

(14) *Solo Singers*: Many British singers, particularly opera singers, now sing in every part of the world. Before the second world war there were scarcely any with an international reputation.

(15) *Opera*: There is no National Opera House, but the Royal Opera House at Covent Garden receives a grant from the Arts Council. It gives performances *throughout the year* of opera and ballet. The English National Opera Company (formerly Sadler's Wells) performs operas, sung in English, at the London Coliseum. It also tours the provinces. The standard of performance is very high. There is an opera season at Glyndebourne, Sussex (May to August). The opera house stands in a beautiful garden. It is fashionable and expensive (evening dress is still worn).

Opera is also performed at many of the arts festivals. And there are many small, but adventurous, opera groups in different parts of the country. Opera in Scotland and Wales is excellent.

(16) *Ballet*: The Royal Ballet Company of Covent Garden is now one of the world's leading ballet companies. There are several other first class ballet companies in Britain.

QUESTIONS

(1) Do you believe that people no longer ask—or care—about a writer's social background?

(2) The writings of the 'Angry Young Men' have been criticised because they are too similar to everyday experience. It is said that people would rather be entertained by unfamiliar situations. Which do you prefer?

(3) 'There is probably a greater interest in painting and sculpture in Britain today than ever before.' Is this also true in your country? If so, why?

(4) What made the Beatles so different from other pop groups?

(5) Do you think that the ideas of the twentieth century can be better expressed in the theatre or the cinema?

FURTHER READING

Evans, I.   A Short History of English Literature
Miller, K. ed.   Writing in England today

Hayward, J. ed.	The Penguin Book of English Verse
Pevsner, N.	The Englishness of Art
Houston, P.	The Contemporary Cinema
Russell Taylor, J.	Anger and After

The last night of the Proms, at the Royal Albert Hall.

*Rock climbing in
the Lake District.*

*The Royal Pavilion at
Brighton.*

14

How the British Spend their Holidays

AT THE SEASIDE

It was the British who started the fashion for seaside holidays—not surprisingly, since nobody in Britain lives more than seventy-five miles from the sea. The trek to the sea began at the end of the eighteenth century, when fashionable London society followed the Prince Regent (later George IV) to Brighton, a small town fifty miles from London (see map p. 214). The prince found the climate agreeable and built himself a summer pavilion there. Today Brighton is a popular place for holiday-makers and the pavilion is used as a museum, picture gallery, assembly room and concert hall. Many Londoners go there for the day during the summer, and Brighton has been called 'London by the sea'.

Gwyn and Mary Williams spend a few days every year at Brighton. They sit on the crowded, stony beach, sleep in the sun, listen to their transistor radio and occasionally have a swim in the sea. In the evenings they go to concerts of light music or funny shows, and they often spend an hour or two on the pier. Piers are a speciality of British seaside towns. They stretch out to sea, carrying on their iron legs restaurants, theatres, dance halls and other places of amusement. Gwyn spends hours putting pennies in slot machines, hoping to win a prize, whilst Mary visits the fortune-teller or has her photograph taken wearing a hat with 'Brighton' painted on it. On their way back to the hotel, they walk under the bright lights of the sea front eating fish and chips out of a newspaper.

Herbert Perkins, being a northener, does not like Brighton.

'It's just a suburb of London,' he says. 'Now take Blackpool! You've never seen anything like the lights of Blackpool! Blackpool's tough— and you know it's *northern* the moment your landlady says "cum in!"'

Blackpool is on the Irish Sea about thirty miles north-west of Manchester. Bus loads of holiday-makers pour into it from all over the north. They come from the midlands, too, and from Scotland and Wales, and even from the south.

'There's plenty of money in Blackpool,' says Herbert. 'I've known Yorkshire miners spend £150 in a week there.'

HOLIDAYS

Last year the Macdonalds decided to spend their summer holiday in Cornwall. Like everyone else, they had booked their hotel rooms months in advance—in January, in fact—since they knew that if they waited until nearer the time there would be no rooms left during July and August, the main holiday period.

They started out early in the morning. The road was good, but it was not a motorway and all the traffic seemed to be going in the same direction—their direction![2] The sun was setting when they finally reached the little seaside town where they were going to stay. Ian, who had been driving, was very tired. He stopped the car outside a small hotel on the sea front (overlooking the sea) and they all got out.

PEGGY: Look at all that sand, children! Tomorrow Daddy will help you build a sandcastle—*two* sandcastles, won't you, Daddy?

IAN: I want my supper—and a wash. Come on! Let's get inside.

HOTEL RECEPTIONIST: Good evening, madam. What can I do for you?

PEGGY: The name's Macdonald. We've booked two double rooms for a week.

RECEPTIONIST: I'm afraid there's been a mistake, madam. Look! You booked for *next* week.

IAN: Oh Lord! I told you not to let Mother do the booking for us!

PEGGY: Haven't you any rooms free at all?

RECEPTIONIST: In August, madam? I'm terribly sorry, but the whole town's booked out. I'm afraid you won't find a room anywhere.

IAN: Not even a bed and breakfast place?

RECEPTIONIST: You might possibly find a farm, if you went inland.

PEGGY: We want to be by the sea—because of the children.

RECEPTIONIST: Then I don't know what to suggest. There's a caravan park two miles along the coast, but I'm sure it's full. Or there's a Butlins holiday camp[6].

IAN: No, thank you! We want some peace and quiet — is there anywhere we can get a meal?

RECEPTIONIST: At this hour? It's already nine o'clock. You could try the next town. The restaurants will be closed, but there are one or two snack bars.

IAN: We've been twelve hours on the road. There were queues five miles long in places. The children are dead tired.

RECEPTIONIST: Well . . . I'm sure we can do something for the children. They can sleep on the sofas in the lounge. But I'm afraid I can't help you and your wife.

PEGGY: Oh, don't worry about us. We can sleep in the car. Cheer up, Ian! The drive home won't be so bad. There won't be nearly so much traffic going back to London!

HITCH-HIKING

Gareth and Christine went youth-hostelling[7] in the Lake District (see map p. 214) last summer, and, since they could not afford the bus or train fare, they decided to hitch-hike. A lorry driver was the first to stop and give them a lift, but he only took them fifty miles. They travelled the next seventy miles in a second lorry and then an elderly couple in a Rover took them another thirty miles. They had travelled 150 miles (240 kms) in five hours.

'Not bad!' said Christine.

But at last their luck ran out. They waited by the roadside for an hour and nobody stopped. It began to rain.

'Go and hide behind that hedge!' Christine told Gareth.

'Why?'

'You'll see!'

Gareth obeyed and Christine stood at the edge of the road with thumb raised. Almost at once a sports car drew up.

'Want a lift, beautiful?'

'Thanks,' said Christine. 'Got room for my boyfriend? Come on, Garry! Jump in!'

THE WEATHER

'What's the forecast?' asked Ian.

'Oh, showers and sunny intervals!' said Peggy. 'But you don't want to believe the forecast!

The British love to complain about the weather. Notice how often they mention it when they greet you. However, there are rarely extremes of cold or heat in Britain and when temperatures drop below 0°C or rise above 32°C nobody is prepared.

There is usually more rain in the west than in the east, and more snow in the north than in the south. But sometimes there are heavy snowfalls in Kent when there is no snow at all in Yorkshire. The Scottish island of Skye may have winter days which are milder than winter days in the south of France.

It is extremely difficult to forecast exactly how much sun or rain any day, week or month will produce, but Britain is not really wetter or less sunny than many other parts of north-western Europe.

SIR ERIC GOES ON A BIRD-WATCHING HOLIDAY IN EAST ANGLIA

Sir Eric lay on the sandhill behind a clump of coarse grass. Behind him the waves of the North Sea were crashing on an empty beach (see map p. 214). A board stuck in the sand warned 'DANGER. NO BATHING'. But Sir Eric was looking inland across the salt marshes. He was alone and there was not a building to be seen on the flat skyline, except a windmill and a lighthouse.

Sir Eric was waiting for the birds—not with a gun, but with a pair of powerful glasses. Birds came to feed on the salt marshes and on the mud flats of the nearby estuary. Sir Eric sometimes waited hours for the sight of a rare bird, but this time his eye was caught by a pair of birds nesting on the sandhills. He watched them through his glasses. The hours passed. When at last he looked up, the salt marshes had disappeared beneath the incoming sea. He got up. The line of sandhills had become an island. Far away he could see a small figure standing on the sand beside a motor-boat. It was Hester. She was used to his absent-mindedness and had come to fetch him.

There are many enthusiastic naturalists in Britain—many people, young and old, who study the habits of animals, plants and insects, and explore the countryside in search of them.

HOLIDAYS ABROAD

Hundreds of thousands of British people—from nearly every income group—can now have cheap holidays of the sort advertised above. Thousands of people tour the Continent in their cars. Thousands of young people hitch-hike or join organised parties or go to work on farms, helping with the harvest, picking fruit, etc. Rich people fly to expensive hotels and villas on the Mediterranean or in the West Indies. There are many sea cruises (some quite cheap) and some L.E.A.s organise very cheap cruises for children.

THE ROAD TO KATMANDU

Susan and Jeremy, with another boy and a girl, are planning a trip next month to the middle East, Afghanistan, India and Nepal. They are going to travel overland, taking buses and hitch-hiking. They will find cheap lodgings wherever they can, and if necessary they will sleep under the stars. They will have very little money. Sir Eric is worried.

'I don't like to think of Susan and that other girl going all that way with two inexperienced boys. How will they manage if anything goes wrong?' he said. 'I'd willingly help to pay for the trip if they'd agree to sleep in decent hotels.'

'You know she won't accept any money from you beyond her allowance,' said Hester. 'Besides, the road to Katmandu is pretty well-worn these days. They'll meet plenty of other young people doing the same trip.'

The longing to get off the beaten track—away from western civilisation—is strong among many young people. Before going up to university and during university holidays, many British students drive, trek and fly into the far corners of Africa and Asia.

NOTES
(1) *Where to go in Britain*

ENGLAND

Dartmoor and Exmoor (Devon and Somerset). There are high, bare, wild hills, rocks and deep wooded valleys with rushing streams containing trout and salmon. Rare wild ponies and red deer can be found on Exmoor, which also has a wild sea coast.

Derbyshire Dales ('dale' is a northern word meaning 'valley'). There are deep, narrow gorges (rocky valleys with steep sides), gentle streams and tall, bare hill tops.

Yorkshire Dales (running east from the Pennines). The features of the countryside are: broad, lonely unspoilt valleys; clear streams with waterfalls; wide views from bare mountain tops. The dales are a mixture of farmland and wild hillsides, with old villages of stone-built houses.

Yoskhire Moors. Here wild heathery hills and deep broad valleys stretch, in some places, as far as the North Sea. The villages are stone-built, like those in the dales.

The Lake District. This is one of England's favourite touring spots, but it is still easy to get away from people. There is an immense variety of mountain, lake and valley scenery, and many high, rocky cliffs. Wordsworth and other Lake poets made this region famous.

The Cheviots. These are the loneliest and wildest hills in England, right on the Scottish border. It is sheep country, and great new forests have been planted, but it is still mostly rolling country of bare hills and streams.

Northumberland. This is wild, rolling country, with historic castles, and a fine coast of sandy beaches. There are stretches of the Roman Wall built by the Emperor Hadrian. It is possible to walk for miles along the top of it, with unspoilt views on either side.

The Cotswolds. The rolling hills here are mostly farmland. The region is famous for ancient, carefully preserved villages and small towns, composed of houses built of golden stone.

The Coast. Apart from a few stretches in Kent and Sussex, the south coast is built-up and spoilt. There are fine white cliffs in Dorset, but the army has kept the most beautiful stretches as a training ground. Most of the Devon, Cornish and Somerset coasts are very fine, with tall cliffs, deep estuaries, woods, old-world towns and fishing villages. Many miles of coastal paths run along the cliff tops of soft grass and heather.

East Anglia. This is the richest plough-land in Britain. It is very flat in parts, rather like Holland. The region has many unspoilt towns and villages, a coast of sandhills and marshes, and is famous for its small lakes (called 'broads').

The River Thames. This river is historic and interesting from its mouth to its source. It is possible to take boat trips from London to Oxford.

The Southern Counties. There is a network of little roads, lanes and footpaths over hills, through farmland and woods. Footpaths are all well signposted. There are many attractive villages, most of them with pubs. Cheap hotels and houses offering bed and breakfast can be found in all small towns.

Off the beaten track. (i.e. away from the main roads). Most counties have unspoilt corners. Many southerners imagine that from Birmingham northwards, English countryside has been completely swallowed by the industrial cities of the Black Country, but there is more wild, unspoilt country in the north than in the south.

WALES

Snowdonia (North Wales). This is very popular mountain country, containing tall, rocky hills, lakes, waterfalls and river estuaries bordered with mountains.

South Wales. The mountains and river valleys (Black Mountains, Brecon Beacons, the Towy Valley) are surprisingly unspoilt, although they are so near the coal-mining districts.

Central Welsh Mountains. This is pleasant, but not grand scenery in a very lonely and underpopulated area. There are sheep farms and newly planted forests.

The Coast. Much of the Welsh coast is beautiful, including most of the Island of Anglesey. The bridge across the Menai Straits, built by Telford in 1819, is one of the oldest suspension bridges in the world. Pembrokeshire has fine cliffs, sandy beaches and islands famous for their birds. Unfortunately it is also well-known for the new oil port at Milford Haven.

SCOTLAND

The Western Highlands. There is magnificent scenery throughout, including mountains covered with purple heather in August. The sea lochs (lakes) and fresh water lochs are bordered by wild mountains. There are very few towns and villages, only a limited number of hotels, and very few roads. This is the country of red deer, wild cats, seals, gannets (the largest northern sea bird), salmon and golden eagles.

The Western Isles (the Hebrides). This is a group of hundreds of islands, large and small: some are flat with sandy beaches, others, like the historic Isle of Skye,

Hadrian's Wall, which defended the northern frontier of Roman Britain.

Typical thatched cottages in England.

The harbour at Polperro, a well-known and beautiful fishing village in Cornwall.

have some of the tallest, rockiest mountains in Britain. Many of the islands can be reached by regular ferry services.

The Eastern Highlands (Cairngorms). This is the highest chain of mountains in Scotland, but they are flat-topped. Because it is drier here than in the Western highlands it makes wonderful walking country. There are broad salmon rivers, and ancient pine forests. A new holiday centre has been established at Aviemore, where skiing is possible in winter.

The Southern Uplands. These are high, lonely hills. Although this region is much less popular than the Highalnds, in parts, especially Galloway, it is very lovely.

Mountain Climbing in Britain: Although no mountain in Britain is higher than 4,406 feet (Ben Nevis in Scotland), there are high, dangerous rock faces on many mountains in England, Wales and Scotland. The mountaineers who first climbed Mount Everest in 1953 trained on the rock faces of Snowdonia in North Wales.

(2) *British roads*: Britain is the only country in Europe (with Malta) where driving is on the left. There are over 1,000 miles of motorway (mostly three-lane, i.e. track). Other roads, even small roads, have excellent surfaces, but they wind. There are, in fact, very few straight stretches. Britain has the highest density of traffic in the world, and so is continuing to build more motorways and dual carriageways (dual carriageways are like motorways, but are not cut off from the ordinary road system. By-passes are being built round villages and historic towns. But it is doubtful that the government will complete its road programme in the 1980s because of the cuts in expenditure made in 1976, resulting from the state of the economy.

The British are, on the whole, careful and considerate drivers, and the accident rate in Britain is one of the lowest in Europe.

(3) *National Parks*: Many of the districts described above (in England and Wales particularly) are National Parks. The land is in private ownership but building is strictly controlled. Owners are encouraged to let visitors walk on their land. Many other districts, too, are protected from 'development' by special government or local authority control.

(4) *Preservation Societies*: There are many of them, large and small. Much the most important is the *National Trust*[5], founded nearly eighty years ago by a group of natural beauty lovers.

(5) *The National Trust*: The National Trust was founded in 1895. The purpose of the organisation is to preserve historic buildings and places of natural beauty in Britain. It gets its money from all kinds of people who give large or small amounts to enable it to carry on its work. The Trust owns large areas of beautiful scenery all over Britain. Its property includes ancient castles, bird sanctuaries (places where people are not allowed to shoot birds or take eggs from

nests), birthplaces and homes of famous people, and fine examples of the architecture of different periods. Since 1946 land and houses of interest to the nation can be given to the National Trust instead of paying death duties. Thanks to the Trust, ordinary people can now see fine collections of paintings, furniture and other valuable objects that they had no chance of seeing before.

(6) *Holiday Camps*: There are holiday camps all round the coast, the most famous being Butlins and Pontins camps. They are ideal places for people who do not want the effort of looking for entertainment. Trained staff look after the children so that the parents can have time off to enjoy themselves. Billy Butlin, the Canadian who started the Butlins camps, is now immensely rich and has been knighted (see p. 28).

(7) *Youth Hostels*: The Youth Hostel Association of England and Wales was founded in 1930. Its aim is 'to help all of limited means (i.e. with little money) to a greater knowledge, care and love of the countryside'. It offers simple and inexpensive accommodation to young holiday-makers when they are touring. There are similar associations in Scotland, Ireland and many other countries, and members of one are admitted to the others.

Membership fees (for one year).

Over 21 years	£1.62p
16–20 years	£1.08p
Under 16	£0.54p

Charges for members from other countries are agreed by the International Youth Hostel Federation.

(8)

HOLIDAYS WITH PAY

	Minimum number of days by law	Minimum number of days by collective agreement	Public holidays
Belgium	18	20-22	10
Denmark	24	24	9.5
France	24	24	8-10
Germany	15-18	18-24	10-13
Ireland	12	18	6
Italy	12	14-20	17-18
Luxembourg	18-24	18-24	10
Netherlands	15-18	17-20	7
UK	Nil	15-18	6-7

QUESTIONS

(1) Some people claim that hitch-hiking is immoral. Do you agree?

(2) Can you explain why the British talk so much about the weather?

(3) Do you think it strange that the British like to spend their holidays by the sea? In what sort of country do you like to spend your holidays?

FURTHER READING

Hoskins, W. G.   The Making of the English Language
Moorhouse, G.   The Other England
Allsop, K.   Fit to live in? *(Connexions)*
B.P.   Map of Great Britain
B.P.   Regional Maps of Great Britain

15

Britain and the Outside World

The Commonwealth of Nations is a 'free association of entirely independent states'. It is not a federation, or union, of states like the United States of America or the USSR. There are no written laws, no elected parliament, no supreme ruler. The British government has no more power over Canada or India than it has over Mexico or China. Elizabeth II is called 'Head of the Commonwealth', and she is still Queen of many of its member countries. But Malaysia and the Pacific island of Tonga have their own sovereigns, and India, Ghana and Cyprus, among others, are republics. Very few of the new Commonwealth countries have kept the British form of parliamentary government.

'Some now have forms of government which they feel suit them better,' Charles said to Carlos one day. 'A lot of British people are surprised and shocked that they don't want our kind of democracy.'

'A lot of the British must be very simple-minded, then!' said Carlos. 'They seem to imagine that British democracy can be transplanted to any part of the world and that it will work just as it does in Britain. They forget that in other countries customs and values are different—and the people are different too!'

The new Commonwealth has grown out of the old British Commonwealth and Empire. In the days of the old Commonwealth the only self-governing nations were Canada, Australia, New Zealand and South Africa. They were known as 'dominions'. Except for the French-speaking Canadians of Quebec and the Afrikaaners of South Africa (who originally came from Holland), the populations of these dom-

223

Two aspects of the Commonwealth: the vast agricultural prairies of Canada, and modern educational aids in use in Zambia.

inions were composed almost entirely of people of British descent. Anne Blakeney, for example, has more Anglo-Saxon blood in her than Charles, one of whose grandmothers was French. The people of the dominions were bound to the mother country only by ties of affection and loyalty, and they fought alongside Britain in both world wars by their own choice. Anne's father was wounded in the second world war, and her grandfather was killed in the first world war.

The old British Commonwealth and Empire came to an end with the second world war. The new Commonwealth was born when Clement Attlee's Labour government granted independence to India and Pakistan in 1947. Since that date both Labour and Conservative governments have systematically granted independence to nearly all the former British colonies and protectorates. The colonies were given a choice. They could break all ties with Britain, or they could remain within the Commonwealth—completely free and self-governing, like the old dominions. The Commonwealth has developed and changed greatly during the last twenty-five years. The great majority of these new independent states have decided to stay in the Commonwealth[1].

On the other hand, in 1961 South Africa left the Commonwealth, because its policy of 'apartheid', separate development for whites and non-whites, made a workable relationship with the New Commonwealth nations impossible. This was also the case with South Africa's neighbour, Rhodesia. Rhodesia cut off its connections with Britain and the Commonwealth, because it was unwilling to carry out the British government's plans for the integration of the African and white populations. In 1965 White Rhodesia illegally declared its independence, and in 1970 became a republic with Ian Smith at its head. (See Note 8.) Pakistan left the Commonwealth when East Pakistan (Bangladesh) successfully rebelled in 1971, with the aid of the Indian government—and army.

'The Commonwealth,' said a former African president, 'is the only world-wide association of peoples in which race, religion and nationality are transcended by (are less important than) a common sense of fellowship'.

Carlos has doubts about this 'common sense of fellowship'.

'There have been wars, civil wars and quarrels in every part of your Commonwealth,' he said to Anne. 'And most of them were an inheritance of your imperial past. How many British people realise, or will admit, that the British Empire, like all empires, was built largely on conquest and exploitation?'

'Oh, quite a lot do,' Anne replied. 'There have been plenty of programmes on TV criticising British imperialism—all imperialism, in fact.'

'I've noticed that some British people are proud that the British Empire broke up without bloodshed,' said Carlos, 'but how long is the Commonwealth which took its place going to last?'

'You mean you don't think it *will* last!' replied Anne. 'Personally I'd be sad to see the Commonwealth break up. It's rather like a club. Membership isn't compulsory, but members can, and often do, give each other help and advice.'

Britain did not put import taxes on Commonwealth goods before she joined the Common Market. But now that she is 'in Europe', this close trading relationship will no longer be the same. However, the Commonwealth seems likely to survive these pressures.

In 1973 Britain gave grants of £183 million to developing Commonwealth countries and £40 million to other developing countries. British and Commonwealth scientists and engineers are working together to improve food production all over the world. In fact, Britain provides more educational and scientific experts for the United Nations Development Programme than any other nation.

'The money and help we give is only a drop in the ocean, of course,' Charles said. 'I sometimes think that we, like all the other affluent nations, are really more interested in building up our markets than in making things easier for the people. We British always have to find a moral reason for what we do. We deceive ourselves, but foreigners see through us. That's why they so often call us hypocrites.'

Views like this shock Susan.

'But Charles, I've got friends who've been to Africa and Asia and worked with the people there! Governments may be hypocritical, but the people who do the actual work certainly aren't.'

'I didn't say they were,' said Charles. 'I think it's wonderful the way young people go out and work in these places. It just saddens me to think that all their efforts may be wasted.'

'Is it a waste of effort to show that just a few people care?'

In London there is a Commonwealth Secretariat. There are more than 250 Commonwealth societies and forty Commonwealth professional associations[3]. The prime ministers, or heads of state—those who wish to—meet every two years or so to hold discussions. Commonwealth citizens continue to come to Britain in large numbers, not only as immigrants, but also as students and visitors. English continues to be the common language of the Commonwealth, and the pound sterling the common currency.

At the same time more and more British people are visiting the Commonwealth countries as tourists. There is also a growing interest, particularly among young people, in the ancient cultures of the Asian and African peoples.

THE BRITISH DECIDE WHERE THEY BELONG

The European Economic Community (EEC), known as the Common Market, came into being in the 1950s. At that time Britain stood apart from the rest of Europe, believing that her future lay with the Commonwealth and in a 'special relationship' with the United States. Britain saw herself as a *world* trading power and did not wish to be hindered by membership of a *European* economic community. British governments, Labour and Conservative, also believed that, in spite of the disappearance of the 'Empire' after the second world war, Britain had a duty to give help and advice to her former colonies. She believed that no other power in Western Europe had such world-wide responsibilities.

Besides, British people of all parties were afraid of finding themselves one day part of a European state, with no proper control over their own affairs. The extremists, or 'Little Englanders', as they were called, weren't going to have foreigners dictate to them on anything whatsoever.

However, in the 1960s Britain applied twice to become a member of the EEC—in 1961–62 under the Conservatives, and in 1967 under Labour Prime Minister, Harold Wilson. Each time the British people were willing, but on both occasions the French President, General de Gaulle, replied, 'Non!'

When the Conservative Prime Minister, Edward Heath, tried again in 1970, pro- and anti-marketeers were bitterly divided, and there were now more anti-marketeers than pro-marketeers. The two main parties were also divided. Only the Liberals were, as ever, solidly pro. Most

Conservative MPs were pro, while most Labour MPs were anti. On both sides, however, there were high-ranking people who disagreed with the majority view of their parties.

Below is the last part of a TV debate (broadcast during the period of negotiations in 1971) for which viewers had sent in their questions beforehand. Some of the viewers were invited to be in the audience and put their questions to the panel:

The Panel—Chairman: Leonard Townsend
         Pro-Common Market
         Mary Lee (Labour M.P.)
         Francis Mann (Conservative M.P.)
         Anti-Common Market
         Bruce Langley (Conservative M.P.)
         Kenneth Wilding (Labour M.P.)

Questioners in the audience:
         Mrs Peggy Macdonald (secretary and housewife)
         Gwyn Williams (factory worker)
         George Clarke (schoolboy, parents Jamaican immigrants)
         Colonel Mannering (army officer, probably retired)

LEONARD TOWNSEND: We've had quite a lot on the economic problems of the Common Market, and we really must move on to look at some of the other aspects. Mrs Peggy Macdonald, can we have your question, which I think concerns some of the Commonwealth countries.

PEGGY MACDONALD: Yes, I'm a secretary as well as a mother and housewife, and I'd like to know why we have to stop buying cheaper products from the Commonwealth like butter and lamb from New Zealand, or sugar from the West Indies. What effect is this going to have on the Commonwealth countries who depend on Britain as their chief market? It seems madness to me.

LEONARD TOWNSEND: Bruce Langley, would you like to go first on this one?

BRUCE LANGLEY: Yes, of course it's madness, complete madness, to push the cost of living up even faster by stopping Commonwealth foodstuffs coming in. Many of the Commonwealth countries are agricultural countries—they have the land and the manpower to grow cheap food, which the industrial countries of Europe don't have; and because they're agricultural countries they'll suffer twice as much if we stop buying from them, despite everything the present government tries to make us believe.

FRANCIS MANN: Oh, really, Bruce, you know as well as I do that's an over-dramatic point of view. After all, New Zealand has the most to lose and yet the New Zealand government has already approved the terms offered to it if Britain goes in. The same applies to the West Indies and their sugar. Britain may be the traditional market for Commonwealth foodstuffs. I'll agree that she's the largest—at the moment. But they're not going to be *stopped* from coming in, and if these Commonwealth countries are given enough time, they'll be able to find plenty of other markets for their goods. That's why there's going to be a five-year change-over period.

BRUCE LANGLEY: Yes, but even if it was as easy as you make it sound, it doesn't answer the question of why the British housewife has to bear the cost.

FRANCIS MANN: Oh, I think the answer to that is very obvious. We can't expect to have the advantages of an increased European industrial market on the one hand, and to deny the six the chance to develop their agricultural industry by selling here. Britain already has an efficient agricultural industry but it can provide only a part of all we need. If we provide continental farmers with a larger market for their produce, they will be able to increase the size of their farms and their output, and bring prices down.

MAN IN THE AUDIENCE: There's something I'd like to ask. If we join...

LEONARD TOWNSEND: Just a minute, sir. Before you ask your question, would you mind telling me your name and what you do.

G. WILLIAMS: All right, I'm Gwyn Williams and I'm a factory worker. What I want to know is will we be free to make our own laws and our own decisions if we join. I mean, will the government still be able to decide what happens in Britain or will someone else tell us what to do?

LEONARD TOWNSEND: Thank you Mr Williams. This is really a question about sovereignty and I know from the letters we've had that this is something which worries a good many people. Mary Lee?

MARY LEE: Yes, I do agree that a lot of people are concerned about this; but really, you know, Mr Williams, you have no need to be. Look at

France. France is a member of the six but she has never followed a Common Market policy if she believed it to be against French interests. There's no reason to expect that Britain will have less freedom . . .

KENNETH WILDING: I don't agree with that at all, and I'm sure the majority of British people don't either. We *will* lose our sovereignty by joining the six—not immediately perhaps, but in the long run. Foreign policy will be affected, so will agriculture and many other things; and, look, if what Mary Lee says is right why has Britain already decided to use metric measurements, and to introduce the value added tax? We're losing our freedom already, and we haven't even joined yet. Once we've signed the Treaty of Rome we shall be on a moving staircase going towards a single European state.

LEONARD TOWNSEND: What about that, Francis Mann? Are we on a one-way ticket towards a single state?

FRANCIS MANN: Not in our lifetime, no, we're not. As far ahead as we can see, I believe we shall have all the advantages of being part of a block without any of the disadvantages. Can I ask Mr Williams if he's a trade unionist?

GWYN WILLIAMS: Yes, I am.

FRANCIS MANN: So you believe in collective strength? You believe that if all the members of a union stand up for something you're more likely to get it than when two or three are standing alone?

GWYN WILLIAMS: Yes, of course. That's what trade unions are all about.

FRANCIS MANN: Exactly. The same argument applies to the countries of Europe. In any case, if you come to think about it you'll realise that there are already dozens of agreements between countries and between blocks of countries. Do you imagine that the governments of any of these countries would act alone, without consulting the others? Of course they wouldn't! The economic difficulties that America, Japan and the European countries have had in the last four or five years prove that. You know the saying 'If America catches a cold, the rest of the world catches pneumonia'. So I believe that our sovereignty in Britain won't really be any more affected than it is now; certainly not in the day-to-day laws, and so on, that affect the man in the street most often. I do think, though, that one day in the very distant future we shall move towards a United States of Europe—and I welcome it.

Edward Heath signs Britain into the Common Market, 23rd January, 1972.

The Commonwealth Games, Edinburgh, 1970.

LEONARD TOWNSEND: Kenneth Wilding, do you want to come back on this?

KENNETH WILDING: Yes, I do. I'm certainly all for unity. Francis Mann used the term 'blocks of countries' and this is exactly what worries me. We've got Eastern blocks and Western blocks. Now we're talking about a Common Market block. And let's remember also that Russia and the Comecon group of states in Eastern Europe are worried by a larger Common Market in Western Europe.

LEONARD TOWNSEND: You mean that they're afraid that this will result in two opposing blocks, with rigid attitudes that are slow to change?

KENNETH WILDING: Yes, that's exactly what I mean, and I don't blame the Russians and their friends for being afraid. I would be very afraid if Europe were divided into two rival blocks.

LEONARD TOWNSEND: You mean there would be a danger of war?

KENNETH WILDING: Well, no! That's exaggerating, but I certainly think that it would increase the risks of war. In any case, it's another good reason for keeping Britain out of the Common Market. I believe that Britain should continue to build up her trade in Europe; that we should retain our independence but continue our special relationship with the USA; and that we should continue to be the chief market for the Commonwealth. If we did this we would maintain the freedom to act as we thought best in any situation.

LEONARD TOWNSEND: I'm glad you mentioned the Commonwealth again, Kenneth Wilding, because our next question is from some-one born in Jamaica, George Clarke, how old are you now?

GEORGE CLARKE: I'm sixteen, and I'm still at school.

LEONARD TOWNSEND: And when did you come to Britain?

GEORGE CLARKE: I came over when I was seven.

LEONARD TOWNSEND: Thank you, can we have your question please?

GEORGE CLARKE: Yes, I want to ask the panel how Britain can suddenly forget the Commonwealth, and what it thinks her relations with the Commonwealth countries will be in the future?

LEONARD TOWNSEND: Thank you George. Well, that's a very blunt question. Mary Lee?

MARY LEE: The answer is just as straightforward as the question. We haven't forgotten the Commonwealth, and it's because we haven't that the negotiations with the six have been so complicated and difficult. In fact, the Caribbean Commonwealth countries, as well as

India, Pakistan and the African Commonwealth countries will all have association with the Common Market if they want it.

BRUCE LANGLEY: Those are just so many words, Mary Lee, as you very well know. Britain's loyalties lie with the Commonwealth, and it is very important for world peace that they should continue to do so. The most important thing about the Commonwealth is that it's multi-racial. It's the only association of its kind in the world—an association in which many races are brought together and in which developing countries have the same rights as developed countries. It's got to survive, but if Britain goes into the Common Market it won't— already the negotiations have done a lot of damage to our relations with the Commonwealth.

FRANCIS MANN: But, Bruce, no Commonwealth country has complained about our trying to become part of Europe. We *are* Europeans. And there is no question of a choice between Europe and the Commonwealth, because Commonwealth countries can trade with the Common Market countries if they wish to. They can become 'associate members'. Indeed, it can make the Commonwealth a stronger multi-racial organisation than it is, and where any real action is concerned it isn't very strong at the moment.

LEONARD TOWNSEND: We could go on with this topic for much longer, but I must interrupt you because time is running short, and we can just get in one more question. The Prime Minister has said that no British government could go into Europe against the wishes of Parliament and the people. Colonel Mannering, I think you have something to say on this point.

COLONEL MANNERING: Indeed I have! I should like to ask the M.P.s on this panel why a referendum should not be held on the question of entry to the Common Market. I suggest it is because the Prime Minister knows very well that if there was a referendum the British people would vote against entry.

LEONARD TOWNSEND: Mary Lee?

MARY LEE: In a few words, the argument against a referendum is, first, that public opinion is always changing. In the middle of 1970 most people would have voted in favour of entry. Now they might well vote against it, as Colonel Mannering says. But who knows what they would vote in a year's time? In other words public opinion swings backwards and forwards very quickly. The second thing is that M.P.s take a great deal of time and trouble to find out all the facts needed to make a decision. Most of the people who would vote in a referendum would be quite incapable of doing this.

LEONARD TOWNSEND: Kenneth Wilding?

KENNETH WILDING: I would just say this—if Denmark, Norway and Iceland can have referendums, why shouldn't we? This is an issue that affects every single person in the United Kingdom, and they should all have the chance to express an opinion.

LEONARD TOWNSEND: Bruce Langley, a quick word to finish?

BRUCE LANGLEY: Although I'm against entry to the Market, I disagree with a referendum in this country. We have a democracy in Britain of which we're proud. This means that the people elect M.P.s to find out all the facts on an issue and to vote on their behalf. As Kenneth says, the Common Market is an issue that affects everyone. It's much too important to be decided by the votes of people who know only half the facts. If the question had been put to a referendum hanging would not have been abolished, but Parliament had more wisdom than the mass of people.

LEONARD TOWNSEND: I must stop you there, Bruce Langley. I'd like to thank you, Mary Lee, Francis Mann, Kenneth Wilding and Bruce Langley for showing us both sides of just a few of the many questions we have to answer before deciding whether to join the Common Market. I'd also like to thank the studio audience for being here and putting their questions to the panel of experts. Thank you and goodnight.

At the third attempt, the French did not say 'No!' and in 1972, Britain, with Ireland and Denmark, signed a Treaty which brought them into the EEC on 1st January 1973.

But the arguments pro and anti continued. They became more heated. The Conservatives were in power. The anti-marketeers, most of whom were Labour, asked whether the government had the right to take the country into the EEC when (according to the opinion polls) most people were anti-EEC. The anti-marketeers also claimed that the price the Conservatives had paid for 'going into Europe' was too high.

When Harold Wilson became Prime Minister again in February 1974, he demanded that the treaty should be re-negotiated. He then promised the British people a referendum if the re-negotiations were satisfactory. Everyone would be able to vote for or against going into Europe.

By March 1975, the re-negotiations were successful. The government was able to tell the British people that it had persuaded the EEC to accept a smaller payment from Britain to the Community bank and to offer British farmers and housewives a better deal. In April the House of Commons voted to stay in the EEC by 396 to 170.

The promised referendum was arranged for 5th June 1975. The pro-marketeers told the people that there would be more markets for British goods in a bigger community, and of course Britain wouldn't lose her independence! The anti-marketeers were more fiery. Britain would lose her independence, and one day a European parliament would interfere with Britain's private affairs. Food prices would shoot up, and our ties with the Commonwealth would be broken. Nobody was wildly excited, not even at the thought of taking part in the first British referendum ever. In the end, the people voted by a 2 to 1 majority to stay in the Common Market.

UNITED AS A KINGDOM?

The future of Great Britain as a United Kingdom is now more in doubt than perhaps at any other time in the past 200 years. While terrorism continues in Northern Ireland, many 'loyalist' Ulstermen are wondering whether they wouldn't be better-off if they broke completely with the UK. Meanwhile, the Scots and the Welsh have felt for a long time that the Parliament at Westminster is basically an English Parliament rather than one representing the UK and they dislike more and more being ruled by Englishmen, especially now that Britain has serious economic and social problems. They wish to deal with their own problems in their own way, particularly the Scots.

Until recently the nationalist parties have been very small. Then suddenly in 1970 the Scottish National Party (SNP) won a seat at Westminster. In the general election of October 1974, the SNP won 11 seats, and about 25% of the Scottish votes. Since then the number of the SNP supporters has doubled. The fact is, there has been an undercurrent of grievance ever since the Scots lost their parliament in 1707 (see p. 53). North Sea oil is only one of their grievances.

The Welsh Nationalist Party (Plaid Cymru) won three seats in the October 1974 election, but none of them in the industrial south. Plaid

Cymru stands for the traditional Wales. It wishes to preserve the old customs and the language of the Welsh. The Welsh as a whole do not want complete independence, but they do want an Assembly in which they can discuss and control their affairs.

The Labour and Conservative Parties have lost so much popularity that the Labour government was forced to listen to the Welsh and Scottish nationalists. The *devolution* of power, the demand for independence by little nations tied to bigger nations, is a peculiarity of the mid-twentieth century.

In November 1975 the Labour government proposed the following:

Scotland should have a law-making assembly of 142 members with a cabinet-type government and a chief minister.

Wales should have an assembly of 72 members, without the power to make laws.

The assemblies should have powers over local government (see p. 82). Both assemblies should receive money grants from Westminster to pay for the services they controlled.

BUT,

There would be no break-up of the United Kingdom. The Westminster government would take action if the assemblies went beyond their powers. The money earned from North Sea oil would go to the UK Exchequer. The Westminster Parliament would continue to control national law and order, regional trade, and general economic and financial (money) policy. Wales and Scotland would not have a separate voice in the various departments of the Common Market.

Some devolution of power is now inevitable, although the Conservatives believe that the Labour plans would lead to the break-up of the UK. The Liberals propose a form of federal government.

Plaid Cymru is not satisfied because the Welsh Assembly would not have the power to deal with the urgent problems of unemployment and housing. The SNP is not satisfied because it wants an independent Scotland, making its own laws and raising all its own taxes.

The United Kingdom entered the Common Market as one kingdom. Whether it remains united or whether its four parts demand separation and go their own way, has now to be decided.

'Well, at least Plaid Cymru and the SNP are not violent,' Ian Macdonald said. 'They haven't killed anyone yet.'

'But will this non-violence last?' Peggy said. 'Some say it can't.'

NOTES

(1) *Remaining British Dependencies*: All the remaining British dependencies combined have (in 1970) a total population of under one million. Each dependency is moving steadily towards complete control of home affairs.

(2) *Trade*: The Commonwealth is responsible for over one-fifth of world trade. One quarter of the total trade of Commonwealth countries is with fellow members.

(3) *Some important Commonwealth organisations*: Colombo Plan for Cooperative Economic Development in South and South-East Asia ('to cooperate' is 'work together with somebody'). Help is given to *all* countries in this region that want it; Special Commonwealth African Assistance Plan; The Commonwealth Scholarship and Fellowship Plan; The Commonwealth Foundation (which arranges interchanges in professional fields); the Commonwealth Parliamentary Association; The Commonwealth Scientific Committee; the Commonwealth Agricultural Bureaux (i.e. offices); the Commonwealth Telecommunications Organisation; The Commonwealth Broadcasting Conference.

In 1970 there were 42,000 Commonwealth students in Britain and at the same time there were 3,000 British teachers, 10,000 technical advisers, 5,000 educational experts in Commonwealth countries. There is also a great deal of interchange of experts and advisers among other Commonwealth countries.

(4) *The Commonwealth Games*: held once every four years, each time in a different part of the Commonwealth. They include athletics, swimming, boxing, wrestling, weight-lifting and cycling. The games are a very popular event, and most Commonwealth countries compete.

(5) *European Economic Community (EEC)*: There are nine member countries of the Common Market—Belgium, France, Italy, Luxembourg, the Netherlands, West Germany, the United Kingdom, Ireland and Denmark. They are politically independent of one another, but they are planning to abolish all customs and trade barriers. No work permits are needed. The Common Market was established in 1957.

(6) *North Atlantic Treaty Organisation (NATO)*: formed in 1949, headquarters Brussels. Twelve member countries: Belgium, Canada, Denmark, France, Iceland, Italy, Luxembourg, the Netherlands, Norway, Portugal, Britain, USA. Greece and Turkey joined in 1952 and Federal Republic of Germany in 1955.

(7) *South East Asia Treaty Organisation (SEATO)*: Member countries—Australia, New Zealand, the Philippines, Thailand, France, Britain, USA. Formed in 1954, headquarters Bangkok.

(8) *Rhodesia*: In 1976 guerrilla bands from liberated Mozambique joined black Rhodesian freedom fighters. There was a call for immediate majority rule. Since there were six million Africans and only 274,000 whites, this would have meant black rule at once. The American Secretary of State, Dr Kissinger, visited Rhodesia and suggested majority rule in two year's time, and equal black and white rule straight away. Ian Smith had to agree, but the African leaders (belonging to four different groups) wanted majority rule at once. In October 1976 the matter was discussed by all the parties at a conference in Geneva, chaired by Britain, and the outcome is not yet known.

QUESTIONS
(1) What would your feelings be if Britain ceased to be a United Kingdom? Give your reasons.
(2) In Britain and the USA there are frequent debates about foreign aid. Do you see this as a duty of the rich countries, or cunning self-interest on their part?
(3) Can you think of anything in favour of empires like the British Empire?
(4) Are you convinced, one way or the other, by the arguments in this chapter about Britain and the Common Market?
(5) Do you think a people should be allowed to govern itself, however badly, rather than be forced to accept government, however good, from another people?

FURTHER READING
Parker, G.	The Logic of Unity (Longman)
Jay, D.	After the Common Market
Uri, P.	From Commonwealth to Common Market
Forster, E. M.	A Passage to India (F)